D0035740

SCHOLASTIC

2023 BOOK OF WORLD RECORDS

BY

CYNTHIA O'BRIEN

ABIGAIL MITCHELL

MICHAEL BRIGHT

DONALD SOMMERVILLE

ANTONIA VAN DER MEER

If you purchased this book without a cover, you should be aware that this book is stolen property. It was reported as "unsold and destroyed" to the publisher, and neither the author nor the publisher has received any payment for this "stripped book."

Copyright © 2022 by Scholastic Inc.

All rights reserved. Published by Scholastic Inc., *Publishers since 1920*. SCHOLASTIC and associated logos are trademarks and/or registered trademarks of Scholastic Inc.

Due to this book's publication date, the majority of statistics are current as of April 2022. The publisher does not have any control over and does not assume any responsibility for author or third-party websites or their content.

No part of this publication may be reproduced, stored in a retrieval system, or transmitted in any form or by any means, electronic, mechanical, photocopying, recording, or otherwise, without written permission of the publisher. For information regarding permission, write to Scholastic Inc., Attention: Permissions Department, 557 Broadway, New York, NY 10012.

This book was created and produced by Toucan Books Limited.
Text: Cynthia O'Brien, Abigail Mitchell, Michael Bright, Donald Sommerville, Antonia van der Meer
Designer: Lee Riches
Editor: Anna Southgate
Proofreader: Marilyn Knowlton
Index: Marie Lorimer
Toucan would like to thank Cian O'Day for picture research.

ISBN 978-1-338-84512-9

10 9 8 7 6 5 4 3 2 1   22 23 24 25 26

Printed in the U.S.A. 40

First printing, 2022

CONTENTS

1

4

MUSIC MAKERS

4

62

SUPER STRUCTURES

7

154

INCREDIBLE EARTH

STAGE & SCREEN
22

ON THE MOVE
46

HIGH TECH
84

AMAZING ANIMALS
110

STATE STATS
180

SPORTS STARS
234

MUSIC MAKERS

TRENDING

#FREEBRITNEY
BRITNEY GETS HER LIFE BACK

Thirty-nine-year-old pop icon Britney Spears made headlines in November 2021 when she was released from a thirteen-year conservatorship—a legal agreement that gave her father control over her life, career, and money. Judge Brenda Penny ruled in Britney's favor, giving her freedom to make her own choices, as well as access to her estate, which is worth about $60 million. Before the hearing, Britney took to Instagram to thank fans for their support with a video of her and fiancé Sam Asghari wearing matching #FreeBritney T-shirts.

#SWIFTTOK
TAYLOR SWIFT JOINS THE APP

TikTok gained a familiar face in August 2021, when Taylor Swift herself posted a nine-second video. The clip, which showed Swift posing in different outfits matching the aesthetic of her recently released albums, was viewed two million times in just three days and prompted one of the featured dresses (representing the album *Fearless*) to fly off store shelves. Since making her debut on the app, Swift has mostly posted about her cats and her re-recorded album, *Red*, gaining her more than eleven million followers as of February 2022.

BLAST FROM THE PAST
ADELE'S EMOTIONAL REUNION

British singing sensation Adele celebrated her career in November 2021 with *An Audience with Adele*, a televised performance and Q&A at the London Palladium. Among the emotional tributes to the star was a surprise appearance by Adele's former English teacher Ms. McDonald, who the singer had previously named as an inspiration. Adele was so overwhelmed by the reunion that she had to leave the stage to fix her makeup.

JUST FRIENDS
CAMILA AND SHAWN BREAK UP

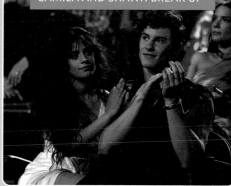

On November 17, 2021, Camila Cabello and Shawn Mendes broke the hearts of "Shawmila" fans with identical posts on Instagram declaring the end of their romantic relationship. The pair, who released the hit "Señorita" in 2019, were together for more than two years, but they had been friends since meeting on tour in 2014. Their joint statement indicated no bad blood between them.

RAIN DOWN FREEDOM
JOHN LEGEND AT THE GRAMMYS

In a bid to raise awareness for the country of Ukraine in its war against Russia, John Legend performed his single "Free" at the Grammy Awards in April 2022. The moving tribute followed a speech given by Ukraine's President Volodymyr Zelensky, in which he urged Americans to "fill the silence with music." Two Ukrainian artists joined Legend onstage: Siuzanna Iglidan, playing a traditional Ukrainian folk instrument—the bandura—and Mika Newton, who sang a verse in Ukrainian.

MOST-STREAMED SONG OF 2021

"DRIVERS LICENSE" OLIVIA RODRIGO

MOST-STREAMED SONGS OF 2021

- **Olivia Rodrigo**, "drivers license"
- **Lil Nas X**, "MONTERO (Call Me By Your Name)"
- **The Kid LAROI** with **Justin Bieber**, "STAY"
- **Olivia Rodrigo**, "good 4 u"
- **Dua Lipa ft. DaBaby**, "Levitating"

Emotions were clearly riding high in 2021—the most-streamed song on Spotify was a runaway victory for Olivia Rodrigo's breakup ballad "drivers license." The *High School Musical: The Musical: The Series* actress stunned the world with her debut single, which was played more than 1.1 billion times according to Spotify's year-end wrap-up. Rodrigo actually took two spots in the streaming giant's top five tracks for the year; "good 4 u," another track from her album *SOUR*, was the fourth-most streamed of the year.

TOP-SELLING ALBUM 2021

30 ADELE

After a six-year hiatus, Adele's much-awaited *30* only took three days to become 2021's top-selling album in the US. Called a "divorce album" by the singer, *30* is actually on track to be Adele's lowest-selling overall and finished the year having sold 1.46 million copies. Her *25*, by contrast, sold 3.38 million copies in the first week alone. Still, *30*'s sales are nonetheless a testament to the singer's enduring popularity; Adele was the only artist with an album passing the million-sales threshold in 2021, and *30* was the best-selling album of any calendar year in the US since 2018!

MOST-LIKED VIDEO ON **YOUTUBE**

"DESPACITO"

With more than forty-seven million likes, "Despacito" is the most-liked video on YouTube. The Puerto Rican dance track by Luis Fonsi feat. Daddy Yankee proved a hot favorite in 2017 and was the first music video to notch up four, five, and then six billion views on YouTube, before hitting an amazing seven billion in October 2020. At that point, the video was being played an average of 1.4 million times a day! That's not to say it's everybody's favorite. According to YouTube's stats, the video is also in the top 20 most-disliked videos on the channel, with more than five million dislikes before YouTube made them invisible.

HIGHEST-GROSSING TOUR ED SHEERAN

British singer-songwriter Ed Sheeran has the highest-grossing tour of all time, surpassing those of U2, the Rolling Stones, Guns N' Roses, and Coldplay. Sheeran's tour for his album ÷ (**Divide**) grossed $775.6 million, making it the biggest moneymaker ever for a musical tour. Sheeran's impressive title is no doubt helped by the fact that the tour stretched for longer than two years, beginning in Turin, Italy, in March 2017 and ending in Ipswich, England, in August 2019. By the time it was over, Sheeran had visited forty-three countries and had performed before 8.5 million people.

HIGHEST-GROSSING ALBUM TOURS

- **Ed Sheeran,** *Divide*
- **U2,** 360°
- **Guns N' Roses,** Not in This Lifetime . . .
- **The Rolling Stones,** A Bigger Bang
- **The Rolling Stones,** No Filter

775.6
736
584.2
558
415.6

FIRST RAPPER TO TOP
BILLBOARD 100 CHART

DRAKE

Drake released his album *If You're Reading This It's Too Late* through iTunes on February 12, 2015. The digital album sold 495,000 units in its first week and entered the *Billboard* 100 at no. 1, making Drake the first rap artist ever to top the chart. The album also helped Drake secure another record: most hits on the *Billboard* 100 at one time. On March 7, 2015, Drake had fourteen hit songs on the chart, matching the record the Beatles have held since 1964. Since releasing his first hit single, "Best I Ever Had," in 2009, Drake has seen many of his singles go multiplatinum, including "Hotline Bling," which sold 41,000 copies in its first week and had eighteen weeks at no. 1 on the *Billboard* 100.

TOP GROUP/DUO

BTS

K-pop megastar band BTS beat AC/DC, AJR, Dan + Shay, and Maroon 5 to be named 2021's Top Group at the *Billboard* Music Awards following another year of global domination. They also took home the awards for Top Song Sales Artist and Top Selling Song (for their hit "Dynamite"), as well as winning Top Social for the fifth year in a row, thanks in part to their infamous "ARMY" of fans around the globe. Their wins at other awards shows in 2021 were no less impressive. They became the first Asian group to win Top Artist at the AMAs and the first K-Pop group nominated for a Grammy.

TOP-SELLING RECORDING GROUP
THE BEATLES

TOP-SELLING RECORDING ARTISTS IN THE UNITED STATES
Albums sold in millions

- The Beatles
- Garth Brooks
- Elvis Presley
- Eagles
- Led Zeppelin

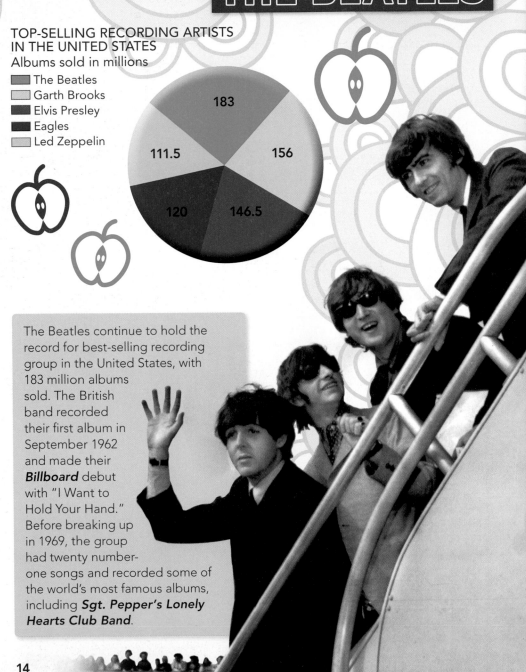

183

156

146.5

120

111.5

The Beatles continue to hold the record for best-selling recording group in the United States, with 183 million albums sold. The British band recorded their first album in September 1962 and made their *Billboard* debut with "I Want to Hold Your Hand." Before breaking up in 1969, the group had twenty number-one songs and recorded some of the world's most famous albums, including *Sgt. Pepper's Lonely Hearts Club Band*.

LONGEST-EVER MUSIC VIDEO

"LEVEL OF CONCERN" TWENTY ONE PILOTS

Twenty One Pilots collaborated with their fans in 2020 to create the longest music video ever! The official video for their hit "Level of Concern" lasted 177 days, 16 hours, 10 minutes, and 25 seconds, with the song constantly looping as fan-made video submissions were played on the live stream. The band announced the end of its "never-ending" stream by joking that the only way it would stop was for the power to go out . . . followed by a video of band member Joshua Dun overloading his Christmas tree with lights!

RICHEST FEMALE SINGER
RIHANNA

Forbes officially named Robyn "Rihanna" Fenty a billionaire in 2021, certifying the Barbadian icon as the richest female singer in the world. Her estimated $1.7 billion net worth doesn't just come from her eight studio albums—$1.4 billion in fact comes from her Fenty Beauty makeup line. With a diverse range of shades for all skin tones and a commitment to cruelty-free production, Rihanna's cosmetics line is a real hit, outshining many other celebrity contributions to the industry.

LONGEST-RUNNING NO. 1 SINGLE

"OLD TOWN ROAD"

From March through July 2019, rapper Lil Nas X's "Old Town Road" spent seventeen weeks in the no. 1 spot, pushing past "Despacito" from Luis Fonsi and Mariah Carey's "One Sweet Day," each of which spent sixteen weeks at the top of the charts. Lil Nas X's real name is Montero Hill, and he is from Atlanta, Georgia. He recorded the song himself, and people first fell in love with the catchy tune on the app TikTok. "Old Town Road" made it to the country charts, but it was later dropped for not being considered a country song. Disagreements about its genre only fueled interest in the song, however, and it subsequently hit no. 1. The song was then remixed and rerecorded with country music star Billy Ray Cyrus, whose wife, Tish, encouraged him to become involved.

MUSIC MAKERS

ACT WITH THE MOST COUNTRY MUSIC AWARDS
GEORGE STRAIT

"King of Country" George Strait won his first two Country Music Awards (CMAs) in 1985 for Male Vocalist of the Year and Album of the Year. Since then, Strait has won an amazing twenty-two CMAs, including Entertainer of the Year in 2013. The country music superstar has thirty-three platinum or multiplatinum albums, and he holds the record for the most platinum certifications in country music. George Strait was inducted into the Country Music Hall of Fame in Nashville, Tennessee, in 2006.

MUSICIAN WITH THE MOST MTV VIDEO MUSIC AWARDS

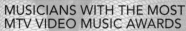

Having been awarded a VMA for best cinematography in 2021 for her video "Brown Skin Girl," Beyoncé is the winningest VMA artist ever, with 30 MTV Video Music Awards. In 2016, Beyoncé tied the record for most VMA wins in one year by a female solo artist, jointly held with Lady Gaga, when she collected eight Moon Person trophies from eleven nominations. The music video for "Formation," from Beyoncé's visual album *Lemonade*, won six awards that year, including the coveted prize for Video of the Year.

MUSICIANS WITH THE MOST MTV VIDEO MUSIC AWARDS

Legend:
- Beyoncé
- Madonna
- Lady Gaga
- Eminem
- Peter Gabriel

30, 20, 18, 13, 13

EL ÚLTIMO TOUR DEL MUNDO BAD BUNNY

FIRST ALL-SPANISH ALBUM TO TOP THE *BILLBOARD* 200 CHART

Bad Bunny's debut album *El Último Tour del Mundo* (*The Last Tour in the World*) made music history in 2020, landing the top spot on *Billboard*'s 200 album chart. It's the first time in *Billboard*'s sixty-four-year history that an album performed entirely in Spanish has reached no. 1. The album, featuring a mix of Latin trap, reggaeton, and ska-punk, was one of three albums released by the Puerto Rican rapper, singer, and songwriter in 2020. His second album, *YHLQMDLG*, made it as high as no. 2 on the chart in March. Bad Bunny, whose birth name is Benito Martínez Ocasio, ended 2020 as Spotify's most-streamed artist of the year, amassing a staggering 8.3 billion streams.

MOST-AWARDED ARTIST
TAYLOR SWIFT

Taylor Swift continues to beat her own records—in 2021, she kept her title as the most-awarded artist ever at the American Music Awards, with two more wins bringing her total to thirty-four. Swift remotely accepted the awards for Favorite Pop Album (for *evermore*) and for Favorite Female Pop Artist. This breaks her record of thirty-two AMAs, set at the 2020 awards. With the next most-awarded artist being Michael Jackson (twenty-six awards), it looks as if it could be some time before Swift's record is beaten . . . by anyone but her, that is! In November 2021, Swift released her own version of her album **Red**, as well as a short film accompanying a ten-minute version of her song "All Too Well."

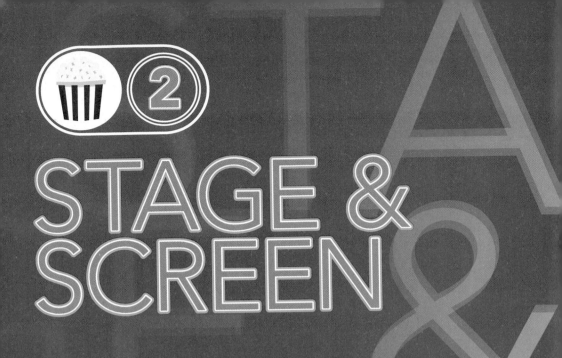

STAGE & SCREEN

2

TRENDING

"THIS IS OUR MOMENT"
TROY KOTSUR AT THE OSCARS

On March 27, 2022, amid a standing ovation and applause in American Sign Language, Troy Kotsur became the second deaf actor ever to win an Oscar at the Academy Awards. He earned the best supporting actor statuette for his role in the film *Coda*, which tells the story of Ruby Rossi, a child of deaf adults (CODA). Kotsur plays her father, Frank. Marlee Matlin, who plays Frank's wife, Jackie, was the first deaf actor to win an Oscar—best actress, for her role in *Children of a Lesser God*, in 1987.

THE MAN? BEHIND THE MASK
KERMIT TAKES A BOW

Masked Singer US had an extra surprise in store in March 2021 when Snail took off the mask to reveal . . . Kermit the Frog. In the show, a celebrity panel tries to guess the identities of singers wearing elaborate costumes, but Kermit's participation marked the first time that the secret star was a character in their own right. Kermit, one of the Muppets, has been played by actor and puppeteer Mark Vogel since 2017.

HAPPY BIRTHDAY, BETTY!
HONORING AN ICON

Hollywood's beloved veteran actress and a lifelong animal rights activist, Betty White passed away on New Year's Eve 2021, just weeks before her 100th birthday. Amid an outpouring of grief, her fans came together to honor her would-be milestone on January 17 with the #BettyWhiteChallenge, making $5 donations to animal shelters and charities in her name.

40 WINS!
AMY SCHNEIDER'S *JEOPARDY!* STREAK

Former Oakland, California, engineering manager Amy Schneider made **Jeopardy!** history with a streak of forty consecutive wins, ending in January 2022. With a huge prize of $1.4 million, she became the second-winningest contestant of all time (after Ken Jennings, with seventy-four games) and the most successful woman ever to appear on the show. Schneider quit her day job soon after her final episode, announcing her intentions to write a book and be a "public figure."

SPIDER-MEN
UNIVERSES COLLIDE IN *NO WAY HOME*

Spider-Man: No Way Home, released in December 2021, was Tom Holland's third Spider-Man movie. While he is not due to stop playing Peter Parker any time soon, **No Way Home** delighted fans of the franchise with the surprise return of former Spider-Man actors Tobey Maguire and Andrew Garfield, who played their own Parker roles as "alternate universe" versions. The two were sworn to secrecy about their cameos, going out of their way to deny return rumors in the buildup to the film's release.

STAGE & SCREEN

LONGEST-RUNNING SCRIPTED TV SHOW IN THE UNITED STATES
THE SIMPSONS

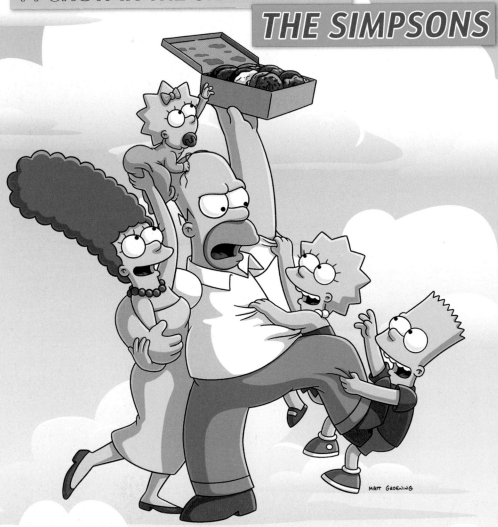

In September 2021, **The Simpsons** entered a record thirty-third season, continuing to hold the title of longest-running American sitcom, cartoon, and scripted prime-time television show in history. The animated comedy, which first aired in December 1989, centers on the antics and everyday lives of the Simpson family. Famous guest stars who have made appearances over the years range from Stephen Hawking to Kelsey Grammer and Ed Sheeran (as Lisa's new crush). Fox has renewed the show for the upcoming thirty-fourth season, too.

TV SHOW WITH THE MOST EMMY AWARDS FOR A COMEDY IN A SINGLE YEAR

SCHITT'S CREEK

Dan and Eugene Levy's hit comedy finished its sixth and final season in 2020, much to the dismay of its fans. However, the Canadian show's successful run was honored on the awards circuit, breaking records by taking home nine Emmys—a new Emmy record for a comedy in a single year! Main cast members Eugene Levy, Catherine O'Hara, Dan Levy, and Annie Murphy won Emmys for Outstanding Lead Actor, Lead Actress, Supporting Actor, and Supporting Actress in a comedy series, respectively, and the show also picked up wins for outstanding writing, casting, costumes, and directing.

MOST POPULAR GAME SHOW

JEOPARDY!

Jeopardy!, which entered its first year without its late host Alex Trebek, was the most-watched show on a syndicated network in 2021, according to Nielsen. It came in ahead of other popular game shows, with **Wheel of Fortune** in second place and **Family Feud** in third. Early episodes in 2021 featured a variety of guest hosts, including Anderson Cooper and LeVar Burton, before Mayim Bialik and *Jeopardy!* champion Ken Jennings took on the cohost roles for a long stint. According to Nielsen, *Jeopardy!* also became the highest-rated program on broadcast and cable TV, not counting sports, in the last week of 2021, as viewers tuned in to watch Amy Schneider's impressive winning streak.

NO. 1 KIDS' MOVIE AT THE US BOX OFFICE

ENCANTO

Disney's newest (and sixtieth ever) animated offering, *Encanto*, had a magical year at the US box office in 2021! Its $91.4 million gross for the year earned it the spot as the number-one kid's movie, and viewers around the world went wild for its catchy songs, penned by Broadway hit maker Lin-Manuel Miranda. *Encanto*, set in Colombia, tells the story of the Madrigal family, who live in a magical house and are blessed with miraculous gifts to help the people of their town.

Yet again, the Super Bowl took the prize for most-watched TV broadcast of 2021—but this time the big game scored less than 100 million viewers. Dropping more than 10 million from 2020's total of 102 million viewers, **Super Bowl LV** attracted 91.6 million people for the Tampa Bay Buccaneers' resounding victory over the Kansas City Chiefs. The 31–9 defeat secured Tom Brady's seventh Super Bowl win, setting a new record, and Brady's team featured in three of the year's top five most-watched broadcasts of 2021.

MOST-WATCHED TELEVISION BROADCAST OF 2021

SUPER BOWL LV

MILLIE BOBBY BROWN

In 2019, Millie Bobby Brown beat Angus T. Jones to become the world's highest-paid child actor. The British actress earned $350,000 for every episode of *Stranger Things* season three, putting her on a level with her adult costars. Her net worth is now reported at around $10 million, thanks to her role in the *Enola Holmes* franchise, modeling work, and various brand endorsements. Brown, a UNICEF Goodwill Ambassador, has donated some of her earnings to help frontline workers during the COVID-19 crisis, and she has raised money for the Olivia Hope Foundation with her makeup line for teens, Florence by Mills. Is there anything this girl can't do?

MOST SUCCESSFUL MOVIE FRANCHISE
MARVEL CINEMATIC UNIVERSE

The Marvel Cinematic Universe franchise has grossed more than $25.5 billion worldwide! This impressive total includes ticket sales from the huge hits of 2018, *Black Panther* and *Avengers*: *Infinity War*. *Black Panther* grossed $1.34 billion worldwide within three months of its release, but then *Avengers*: *Infinity War* hit the screens, taking $1.82 billion worldwide in its first month. With *Avengers: Endgame* earning even greater revenues in 2019, as well as the successful launch of Marvel's Phase Four in 2021 and continued excitement for the franchise, the Marvel Cinematic Universe looks set to hold this record for the foreseeable future.

MOST SUCCESSFUL MOVIE FRANCHISES
Total worldwide gross, in billions of US dollars (as of April 2021)

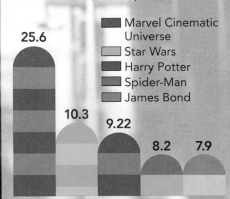

- Marvel Cinematic Universe
- Star Wars
- Harry Potter
- Spider-Man
- James Bond

25.6
10.3
9.22
8.2
7.9

FIRST WOMAN OF COLOR TO WIN BEST DIRECTOR AT THE OSCARS
CHLOÉ ZHAO

Chinese American filmmaker Chloé Zhao made Oscar history at the 2021 Academy Awards, becoming the first woman of color ever to win the Best Director award. Her film, *Nomadland*, tells the story of a middle-aged woman forced to live on the road after losing her home. The woman is played by Frances McDormand, who also won an Oscar for her performance. Zhao was born in Beijing, China, and lived in the UK before moving to the US permanently in her teens. Her success at this year's awards marks only the second time that a woman has won an Oscar for Best Director. The first woman to claim the prize was Kathryn Bigelow for her 2008 film, *The Hurt Locker.*

QUVENZHANÉ WALLIS
YOUNGEST ACTRESS NOMINATED FOR AN OSCAR

At nine years old, Quvenzhané Wallis became the youngest-ever Academy Award nominee for Best Actress. The actress received the nomination in 2013 for her role as Hushpuppy in *Beasts of the Southern Wild*. Although Wallis did not win the Oscar, she went on to gain forty-one more nominations and win twenty-four awards at various industry awards shows. In 2015, she received a Golden Globe Best Actress nomination for her role in *Annie*. Wallis was five years old when she auditioned for Hushpuppy (the minimum age was six), and she won the part over four thousand other candidates.

YOUNGEST ACTOR NOMINATED FOR AN OSCAR
JUSTIN HENRY

Justin Henry was just eight years old when he received a Best Supporting Actor nomination in 1980, for a role he played at age seven. His neighbor, a casting director, suggested that Henry try out for the part. Although the young actor lost out on the Oscar, *Kramer vs. Kramer* won several, including Best Actor for Dustin Hoffman, Best Actress in a Supporting Role for Meryl Streep, and Best Picture. Justin Henry appeared in a few other films before leaving acting to finish his education. He returned to acting in the 1990s.

TOP-EARNING KID YOUTUBER
NASTYA

Anastasia Radzinskaya, better known as Nastya, a seven-year-old Russian girl now living in Florida, became the top-earning child YouTuber in 2021 with an amazing $28 million. Her channel offers an original take on educational and playful storytelling, with content in a number of languages. Nastya now has fifteen separate channels—and her main channel has 90 million subscribers. Her earnings put her ahead of 2020's highest-earning YouTuber, Ryan Kaji, who earned $27 million in 2021 at the age of ten.

MOST POPULAR YOUTUBE CHANNEL
COCOMELON

The preschoolers are taking over! CoComelon Nursery Rhymes, a channel with colorful animated nursery rhymes, became the most-viewed YouTube channel in the United States in 2021 and the top global channel in English. Originally started as a hobby by two parents in Orange County, California, the popular channel ended 2021 with 828.8 million weekly views, 126 million subscribers, and earnings of over $100 million for the year. The channel's most-watched video, "Bath Song," was uploaded in May 2018 and has over 4.9 billion views . . . that's a lot of baths!

JULIA ROBERTS

JENNIFER LAWRENCE

TOP-EARNING ACTRESSES

Actresses Jennifer Lawrence and Julia Roberts tied for the highest per-film salary for an actress in 2021, earning $25 million each for Netflix projects *Don't Look Up* and *Leave the World Behind*, respectively. *Don't Look Up*, which parodies how a celebrity-obsessed world would react to a planet-ending asteroid, was released on the streaming service in December 2021. Although Lawrence was the top-billed actor on the movie, her costar Leonardo DiCaprio made more money on the picture, with a salary of $30 million.

HIGHEST-PAID ACTOR
DANIEL CRAIG

The year 2021's top-earning actor was none other than James Bond himself, with Daniel Craig's final film as the legendary spy, *No Time to Die*, premiering in the fall. But it was Craig's new deal with Netflix for *Knives Out 2* and *3* that netted him a historic $100 million—possibly the biggest single payday an actor has ever received. Craig, who played the Southern detective Benoit Blanc in the first film, is the only actor who will reprise his role in the sequels.

TOP-GROSSING US MOVIE

SPIDER-MAN: NO WAY HOME

TOP-GROSSING US MOVIES OF 2021
In millions of US dollars
(domestic total)

- Spider-Man: No Way Home
- Shang-Chi and the Legend of the Ten Rings
- Venom: Let There Be Carnage
- Black Widow
- F9: The Fast Saga

$613.6

$224.5

$212.6

$183.6 $173

Marvel had another fantastic year, with four of the five top-grossing films of 2021 sitting within the Marvel Cinematic Universe. *Spider-Man: No Way Home* was released in December but still managed to earn $613.6 million in the US and a huge $1.37 billion worldwide. *No Way Home* delighted Spider-fans with appearances from two former iterations of the masked hero, with—spoiler alert!—Tobey Maguire and Andrew Garfield stepping back into the iconic role as alternate-universe versions of Tom Holland's Peter Parker.

Following the 2017 release of the third movie in the series, **Despicable Me 3**, and with a global total of $3.71 billion, **Despicable Me** remains the world's highest-grossing animated franchise of all time. The 2015 spin-off, **Minions**, is the most profitable animated film in Universal Studios' history and was the highest-grossing film of the year, while **Despicable Me 3** and Oscar-nominated **Despicable Me 2** hit spot no. 2 in their respective years of release. Collectively, the four movies beat the **Shrek** franchise's earnings of $3.55 billion. In 2019, **Frozen II** became the biggest-selling animated movie ever with earnings of $1.45 billion worldwide.

LONGEST-RUNNING BROADWAY SHOW
THE PHANTOM OF THE OPERA

Andrew Lloyd Webber's *The Phantom of the Opera* opened on Broadway in January 1988 and has been performed more than 13,500 times. The story, based on a novel written in 1911 by French author Gaston Leroux, tells the tragic tale of the phantom and his love for an opera singer, Christine. All Broadway performances were put on hold during the COVID-19 pandemic, but theaters were up and running again in the fall of 2021.

LONGEST-RUNNING BROADWAY SHOWS
Total performances (as of March 2022)

- The Phantom of the Opera
- Chicago (1996 revival)
- The Lion King
- Cats
- Les Misérables

13,509

9,866

9,480

7,485

7,018

HIGHEST-GROSSING BROADWAY MUSICAL
THE LION KING

Since opening on November 13, 1997, *The Lion King* has earned $1.7 billion. It's Broadway's third-longest-running production and is an adaptation of the hugely popular Disney animated film. Along with hit songs from the movie such as "Circle of Life" and "Hakuna Matata," the show includes new compositions by South African composer Lebo M. and others. The Broadway show features songs in six African languages, including Swahili and Congolese. Since it opened, *The Lion King* has attracted audiences totaling over one hundred million people.

MUSICAL WITH THE MOST TONY AWARD NOMINATIONS

HAMILTON

Lin-Manuel Miranda's musical biography of Founding Father Alexander Hamilton racked up sixteen Tony Award nominations to unseat the previous record holders, **The Producers** and **Billy Elliot: The Musical**, both of which had fifteen. The megahit hip-hop musical, which was inspired by historian Ron Chernow's biography of the first secretary of the treasury, portrays the Founding Fathers of the United States engaging in rap battles over issues such as the national debt and the French Revolution. **Hamilton** won eleven Tonys at the 2016 ceremony—one shy of **The Producers**, which retains the record for most Tony wins with twelve. **Hamilton**'s Broadway success paved the way for the show to open in Chicago in 2016, with a touring show and a London production following in 2017.

YOUNGEST WINNER OF A LAURENCE OLIVIER AWARD

In 2012, four actresses shared an Olivier Award for their roles in the British production of *Matilda*. Eleanor Worthington-Cox, Cleo Demetriou, Kerry Ingram, and Sophia Kiely all won the award for Best Actress in a Musical. Of the four actresses, Worthington-Cox, age ten, was the youngest by a few weeks. Each actress portraying *Matilda* performs two shows a week. In the United States, the four *Matilda* actresses won a special Tony Honors for Excellence in the Theatre in 2013. *Matilda*, inspired by the book by Roald Dahl, won a record seven Olivier Awards in 2012.

ELEANOR WORTHINGTON-COX CLEO DEMETRIOU KERRY INGRAM SOPHIA KIELY

ON THE MOVE

③

TRENDING

UP, UP, AND AWAY
FIRST HELICOPTER FLIGHT ON MARS

On April 19, 2021, NASA's Ingenuity helicopter made the first-ever powered flight on another planet. Having hitched a ride to Mars on the Perseverance rover, it proceeded to make seventeen flights on the Red Planet over the course of 2021. Initially intended just to prove Mars flight was possible, Ingenuity outlasted its projected running time and functioned so well that it was put to work scouting for Perseverance.

BLOCKED!
CONTAINER SHIP GETS STUCK

Global trade was disrupted in March 2021 when **Ever Given**, a 1,300-foot-long container ship, became stuck in the Suez Canal, a waterway connecting the Mediterranean and Red Seas. The **Ever Given** was wedged in the canal for six days, blocking ships from taking the fast route between Europe and Asia. Social media users posted hilarious memes of the massive ship beside the small diggers trying to set it free.

THREE'S A CROWD
MARS MISSIONS REACH ORBIT

Not one, not two, but three different space missions arrived at Mars in February 2021—all in the course of ten days! The first to arrive, on February 9, was an orbiter named Hope, from the United Arab Emirates. Tianwen-1, a Chinese mission made up of an orbiter and a rover, arrived in Mars's orbit on February 10. Finally, NASA's Perseverance rover landed on Mars's Jezero Crater on February 18 and began an exciting search for signs of life.

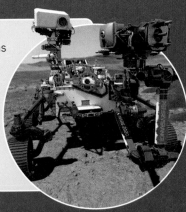

OUT OF THIS WORLD
SPACE TOURISM TAKES OFF

An astronomical year for space tourism, 2021 saw billionaires Richard Branson and Jeff Bezos put on their space suits for privately funded trips. Branson's SpaceShipTwo reached 50 miles above Earth, while Bezos's New Shepard rocket went all the way past the Kármán line—62 miles above Earth! New Shepard made a second trip carrying ninety-year-old *Star Trek* actor William Shatner, the oldest man ever to go to space.

FLYING SOLO
YOUNGEST WOMAN TO CIRCUMNAVIGATE THE GLOBE

At just nineteen years old, Zara Rutherford became the youngest woman ever to fly solo around the world, beating the previous record holder by eleven years. Rutherford took to the skies alone in a Shark Ultra Light plane and documented her journey on social media, stopping in forty-one countries across five continents before landing back in her starting country of Belgium in January 2022, making the journey in 155 days.

WORLD'S FIRST
MONSTER SCHOOL BUS

"Bad to the Bone" was the first monster school bus in the world. This revamped 1956 yellow bus is 13 feet tall, thanks to massive tires with 25-inch rims. The oversize bus weighs 19,000 pounds and is a favorite ride at charity events in California. But don't expect to get anywhere in a hurry—this "Kool Bus" is not built for speed and goes a maximum of just 7 miles per hour.

MOST EXPENSIVE MODERN STREET-LEGAL CAR

BOAT TAIL

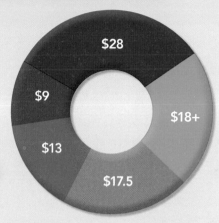

$28

$9

$18+

$13

$17.5

MOST EXPENSIVE MODERN STREET-LEGAL CARS
In millions of US dollars

- ■ Rolls-Royce Boat Tail
- ■ Bugatti La Voiture Noire
- ■ Pagani Zonda HP Barchetta
- ■ Rolls-Royce Sweptail
- ■ Bugatti Centodieci

Unveiled in May 2021, and with a whopping price tag of $28 million, the Rolls-Royce Boat Tail has knocked Bugatti's La Voiture Noire off the top spot to become the world's most expensive street-legal car. One of just three to be produced, the Boat Tail was built to order by the manufacturer's bespoke Coachbuild division. With a sleek design inspired by luxury yachts of the early twentieth century, the convertible grand touring car has a trunk that opens like a pair of butterfly wings to reveal luxury picnicking accessories that include a fridge stocked with the finest champagne!

51

WORLD'S LONGEST MONSTER TRUCK
SIN CITY HUSTLER

Measuring 32 feet in length, 12 feet tall, and weighing 15,000 pounds, the Sin City Hustler is the world's longest monster truck. To put that into perspective, its measurements rival those of a *Tyrannosaurus rex*! The truck was custom-built by Brad and Jen Campbell of Big Toyz Racing in White Hills, Arizona, and currently resides in Las Vegas, Nevada. There, it is used as a tourist attraction. Twelve passengers can climb on board for the wildest drive of their lives!

QTVAN

The tiny QTvan is just over 7 feet long, 2.5 feet wide, and 5 feet tall. Inside, however, it has a full-size single bed, a kettle for boiling water, and a 19-inch TV. The Environmental Transport Association (ETA) in Britain sponsored the invention of the minitrailer, which was designed to be pulled by a mobility scooter. The ETA recommends the QTvan for short trips only, since mobility scooters have a top speed of 6 miles per hour, at best.

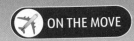

FASTEST LAND VEHICLE
THRUST SSC

The world's fastest car is the Thrust SSC, which reached a speed of 763 miles per hour on October 15, 1997, in the Black Rock Desert of Nevada. **SSC** stands for supersonic (faster than the speed of sound). The Thrust SSC's amazing speed comes from two jet engines with 110,000 brake horsepower. That's as much as 145 Formula One race cars. The British-made car uses about 5 gallons of jet fuel in one second and takes just five seconds to reach its top speed. At that speed, the Thrust SSC could travel from New York City to San Francisco in less than four hours. More recently, another British manufacturer has developed a new supersonic car, the Bloodhound, with a projected speed of 1,000 miles per hour. If it reaches that, it will set a new world record.

FASTEST PASSENGER TRAIN
SHANGHAI MAGLEV

The Shanghai Maglev, which runs between Shanghai Pudong International Airport and the outskirts of Shanghai, is currently the fastest passenger train in the world. The service reaches speeds of 268 miles per hour, covering the 19-mile distance in seven minutes and twenty seconds. *Maglev* is short for magnetic levitation, as the train moves by floating on magnets rather than with wheels on a track. Other high-speed trains, such as Japan's SCMaglev, may have reached higher speeds in testing (375 miles per hour), but are capped at 200 miles per hour when carrying passengers.

268 mph

236 mph

224 mph

217 mph

217 mph

FASTEST PASSENGER TRAINS
(by maximum operating speed)

- Shanghai Maglev
- China Harmony
- Italy Italo
- Spain Velaro
- Spain Talgo 350

FASTEST UNPILOTED PLANE X-43A

In November 2004, NASA launched its experimental X-43A plane for a test flight over the Pacific Ocean. The X-43A plane reached Mach 9.6, which is more than nine times the speed of sound and nearly 7,000 miles per hour. A B-52 aircraft carried the X-43A and a Pegasus rocket booster into the air, releasing them at 40,000 feet. At that point, the booster—essentially a fuel-packed engine—ignited, blasting the unpiloted X-43A higher and faster, before separating from the plane. The plane continued to fly for several minutes at 110,000 feet, before crashing (intentionally) into the ocean.

PARKER SOLAR PROBE

On November 21, 2021, and traveling at 364,621 miles per hour, the Parker Solar Probe set a new record for the fastest human-made object ever known. Jointly operated by NASA and Johns Hopkins University, and equipped with a wide range of scientific equipment, the Parker Solar Probe is on a seven-year mission to study the Sun's atmosphere. Withstanding extreme heat and radiation, it sends data and images back to Earth, revolutionizing our understanding of the star at the heart of our solar system. Also on November 21, 2021, the probe shattered a second record, having reached a distance of 5.3 million miles from the Sun's surface—the closest a spacecraft has ever been, and less than one-tenth of the distance between the Sun and Earth.

APOLLO 10

NASA's Apollo 10 spacecraft reached its top speed on its descent to Earth, hurtling through the atmosphere at 24,816 miles per hour and splashing down on May 26, 1969. The spacecraft's crew had traveled faster than anyone on Earth. The mission was a "dress rehearsal" for the first moon landing by Apollo 11, two months later. The Apollo 10 spacecraft consisted of a Command and Service Module, called Charlie Brown, and a Lunar Module, called Snoopy. Today, Charlie Brown is on display at the Science Museum in London, England.

APOLLO 10 FLIGHT STATS

05/18/1969
LAUNCH DATE

12:49 p.m. EDT
LAUNCH

05/21/1969
DATE ENTERED LUNAR ORBIT

192:03:23
DURATION OF MISSION:
192 hours, 3 minutes, 23 seconds

05/26/1969
RETURN DATE

12:52 p.m. EDT
SPLASHDOWN

LIFTOFF

The Apollo 10 spacecraft was launched from Cape Canaveral, known as Cape Kennedy at the time. It was the fourth crewed Apollo launch in seven months.

LIFTOFF!

FASTEST ROLLER COASTER
FORMULA ROSSA

Thrill seekers hurtle along the Formula Rossa track at 149.1 miles per hour. The high-speed roller coaster is part of Ferrari World in Abu Dhabi, United Arab Emirates. Ferrari World also features the world's largest indoor theme park, at 1.5 million square feet. The Formula Rossa roller coaster seats are red Ferrari-shaped cars that travel from 0 to 62 miles per hour in just two seconds—as fast as a race car. The ride's G-force is so extreme that passengers must wear goggles to protect their eyes. G-force acts on a body due to acceleration and gravity. People can withstand 6 to 8 Gs for short periods. The Formula Rossa G-force is 4.8 Gs during acceleration and 1.7 Gs at maximum speed.

Formula Rossa
World Records
Speed: 149.1 mph
G-force: 1.7 Gs
Acceleration: 4.8 Gs

149.1mph

128mph

120mph

112mph

FASTEST ROLLER COASTERS

- Formula Rossa, Abu Dhabi, UAE
- Kingda Ka, New Jersey, US
- Top Thrill Dragster, Ohio, US
- Do-dodonpa, Yamanashi, Japan
- Red Force, Ferrari Land, Tarragona, Spain

TALLEST WATER COASTER
TSUNAMI SURGE

Rising 86 feet above Hurricane Harbor Chicago amusement park, Tsunami Surge is the tallest water coaster in the world. Psychedelic visual effects light the way as thrill seekers are blasted through 950 feet of slides, tunnels, and hairpin bends at top speeds of 28 miles per hour. This new attraction—the twenty-fifth to debut at the Six Flags park—uses the latest technology in jet propulsion to power its passengers all the way up the steepest slopes . . . and down again.

SUPER STRUCTURES

TRENDING

DESERT DREAMING
THE CITY OF THE FUTURE

In 2021, billionaire Marc Lore revealed plans to build a new American city—right in the middle of the desert! His dream city of Telosa would be home to five million people, and would incorporate eco-friendly architecture, sustainable energy, and a drought-resistant water system. Projecting costs of around $400 billion, Lore and architects from Bjarke Ingels Group are hoping to build the futuristic city by 2030—watch this space!

DRAMATIC DESIGN
GUANGZHOU'S NEWEST THEATER

With bright red curves and delicate gold patterns, the Sunac Guangzhou Grand Theater in China is one of 2021's most beautiful new structures. Inspired by the region's history of silk, the theater was designed by London-based Steven Chilton Architects, and it incorporates drawings by Chinese artist Zhang Hongfei illustrating a local myth—"100 Birds Paying Homage to the Phoenix."

GREENEST TOMATOES
MOREHEAD'S MEGA-GREENHOUSE

Morehead, Kentucky, is home to the United States' biggest greenhouse! AppHarvest's complex has 2.75 million square feet dedicated to growing tomatoes indoors. They are grown hydroponically, which requires 90 percent less water per tomato compared with soil-based methods, making it more environmentally friendly. The conditions in the greenhouse are regulated using technology.

WONDERFUL WOOD
ECO-ARCHITECTURE GETS SMARTER

The city of Skellefteå, Sweden, is known for running on 100 percent renewable energy, and for using wood to build almost everything. New in 2021 is the Sara Cultural Center, a twenty-floor "plyscraper" made out of timber sourced from the local forests. To reduce its carbon footprint, the building gets its energy from solar panels and uses artificial intelligence to control energy and heating, making it a real "climate-smart" creation!

THE FUTURE IS BRIGHT
NEW INUIT ART CENTER OPENS

The Canadian city of Winnipeg, Manitoba, welcomed a new museum in 2021 with the opening of Qaumajuq, a center for Inuit art. Designed by Michael Maltzan, the museum looks like it has been carved from ice, and it has monumental sculptural walls that the architect calls a tribute to the dramatic geographical features often seen around Inuit towns. Qaumajuq, whose name means "it is bright," holds close to 14,000 pieces of Inuit art.

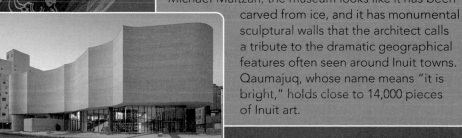

CITY WITH THE MOST SKYSCRAPERS

HONG KONG

CITIES WITH THE MOST SKYSCRAPERS
Number of skyscrapers at 500 feet or higher

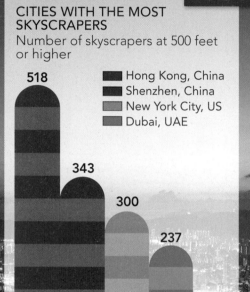

518 — Hong Kong, China
343
300
237

- Hong Kong, China
- Shenzhen, China
- New York City, US
- Dubai, UAE

Hong Kong, China, has 518 buildings that reach 500 feet or higher, and twenty-nine under construction. Six of the buildings are 1,000 feet or higher. The tallest three are the International Commerce Centre (ICC) at 1,588 feet; Two International Finance Centre at 1,352 feet; and Central Plaza at 1,227 feet. Hong Kong's stunning skyline towers above Victoria Harbour. Most of its tallest buildings are on Hong Kong Island, although the other side of the harbor, Kowloon, is growing. Every night a light, laser, and sound show called "A Symphony of Lights" illuminates the sky against a backdrop of about forty of Hong Kong's skyscrapers.

RUNGRADO 1st OF MAY STADIUM

It took over two years to build Rungrado 1st of May Stadium, a huge sports venue that has a capacity for up to 150,000 people. The 197-foot-tall stadium opened in 1989 on Rungra Island in North Korea's capital, Pyongyang. The stadium hosts international soccer matches on its natural grass pitch and has other facilities such as an indoor swimming pool, training halls, and a 1,312-foot rubberized running track. A newcomer to the list, the second-largest venue, India's Narendra Modi Stadium, was inaugurated in 2020.

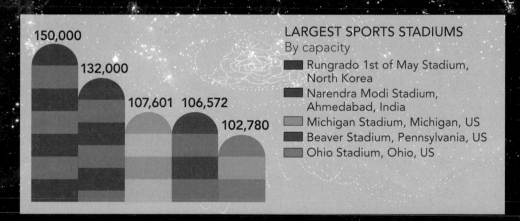

150,000

132,000

107,601 106,572

102,780

LARGEST SPORTS STADIUMS
By capacity

- Rungrado 1st of May Stadium, North Korea
- Narendra Modi Stadium, Ahmedabad, India
- Michigan Stadium, Michigan, US
- Beaver Stadium, Pennsylvania, US
- Ohio Stadium, Ohio, US

WORLD'S MOST EXPENSIVE HOTEL
LOVER'S DEEP

A new contender for the world's most expensive hotel emerged—or rather, **sub**merged—in 2021. The spectacular **Lover's Deep** is a luxury submarine that spends the night touring the underwater world of St. Lucia in the Caribbean Sea. Attended by their own personal butler, guests sleep in spacious quarters full of extravagant furnishings, including a minibar area. As they sit back and relax, huge wraparound windows provide an ever-changing view of the colorful marine life outside. And the cost? Packages vary, but guests booking into the submarine can expect to spend a minimum of $235,000 for just one night.

WORLD'S FIRST HOTEL MADE OF SALT
PALACIO DE SAL

Hotel Palacio de Sal in Uyuni, Bolivia, is the first hotel in the world made completely out of salt. Originally built in 1998, construction began on the new Palacio de Sal in 2004. The hotel overlooks the biggest salt flat in the world, Salar de Uyuni, which covers 4,086 square miles. Builders used around one million blocks of salt to create the hotel walls, floors, ceilings, and furniture. Some of the hotel's thirty rooms have igloo-shaped roofs. The salt flats lie in an area once covered by Lago Minchin, an ancient salt lake. When the lake dried up, it left salt pans, one of which was the Salar de Uyuni.

ANOTHER STRANGE PLACE TO STAY

Hotel shaped like a dog: Dog Bark Park Inn in Cottonwood, Idaho, where you can sleep inside a wooden beagle that measures 33 feet tall and 16 feet wide.

BURJ KHALIFA

Holding the record for the world's tallest building since January 2010, the Burj Khalifa is 2,716.5 feet tall. It not only qualifies as the world's tallest building, but also the tallest human-made structure, the tallest free-standing structure, having the largest number of stories, and the highest aluminum and glass facades (which incidentally cover the same area as twenty-five football fields). The tower took six years to build from start to finish, with 12,000 men on-site day after day, completing twenty-two million hours of work. Dubbed a "vertical city" the tower holds around 10,000 people at any given time.

DUBAI'S BURJ KHALIFA WORLD RECORDS:

1,654 FEET Tallest elevator inside a building

163 FLOORS

1,448 FEET Highest restaurant from ground level

TOUGH CLIMB

No fewer than 2,909 steps lead up to floor 160 of the Burj Khalifa. Anyone wishing to go higher has to do so climbing ladders.

Going up!

NEW CENTURY GLOBAL CENTER

WORLD'S LARGEST FREESTANDING BUILDING

The New Century Global Center in Chengdu, southwestern China, is an enormous 18.9 million square feet. That's nearly three times the size of the Pentagon, in Arlington, Virginia. Completed in 2013, the structure is 328 feet tall, 1,640 feet long, and 1,312 feet deep. The building houses a 4.3-million-square-foot shopping mall, two hotels, an Olympic-size ice rink, a fourteen-screen IMAX cinema complex, and offices. It even has its own Paradise Island, a beach resort complete with artificial sun.

CITYSTARS POOL

Citystars Sharm El Sheikh lagoon, in Egypt, stretches over 30 acres. It was created by Crystal Lagoons, the same company that built the former record holder at San Alfonso del Mar in Chile. The lagoon at Sharm el-Sheikh cost $5.5 million to create and is designed to be sustainable, using salt water from local underground aquifers. The creators purify this water not just for recreation, but also to provide clean, fresh water to the surrounding community.

19.7

30

17.8

1.9   2.2

LARGEST SWIMMING POOLS
Size in acres

- Citystars Sharm El Sheikh, Egypt
- San Alfonso del Mar, Algarrobo, Chile
- MahaSamutr, Hua Hin, Thailand
- Dreamworld Fun Lagoon, Karachi, Pakistan
- Piscine Alfred Nakache, Toulouse, France

WORLD'S LONGEST BRIDGE

DANYANG-KUNSHAN GRAND BRIDGE

Crossing the floodplain of China's Yangtze River, a terrain of hills, lakes, flatlands, and rice paddies, the 102-mile-long Danyang-Kunshan Grand Bridge is the longest bridge in the world. It is a viaduct, which means it is built using many short spans rather than one long one. The spans are raised 328 feet above the ground, on average, and are supported on 2,000 pillars. It's a design that helps the high-speed rail bridge to cross the ever-changing landscape between the Chinese cities of Shanghai and Nanjing. Costing $8.5 billion to construct, the bridge took four years to build using a task force of 10,000 laborers.

COPENHAGEN

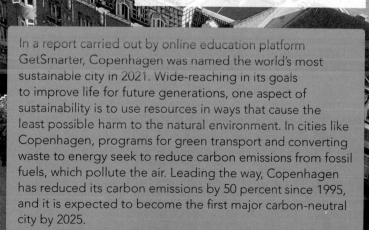

WORLD'S MOST SUSTAINABLE CITIES, 2021

- Copenhagen, Denmark
- Frankfurt, Germany
- San Francisco, CA, US
- Reykjavík, Iceland
- Singapore

In a report carried out by online education platform GetSmarter, Copenhagen was named the world's most sustainable city in 2021. Wide-reaching in its goals to improve life for future generations, one aspect of sustainability is to use resources in ways that cause the least possible harm to the natural environment. In cities like Copenhagen, programs for green transport and converting waste to energy seek to reduce carbon emissions from fossil fuels, which pollute the air. Leading the way, Copenhagen has reduced its carbon emissions by 50 percent since 1995, and it is expected to become the first major carbon-neutral city by 2025.

WORLD'S BIGGEST VERTICAL GARDEN
SANTALAIA BUILDING
BOGOTÁ, COLOMBIA

Completed in 2015, a vertical garden in Bogotá, Colombia, is the largest in the world. Known locally as the "green heart of Bogotá," the garden scales nine of the eleven stories of Santalaia residential building in the Rosales neighborhood of the city, and covers the facade in strips of green that alternate with the windows. Using a system developed by Spanish company Paisajismo Urbano, the green walls cover 33,551 square feet of garden in total—that's almost the size of twelve tennis courts. Beyond being beautiful, vertical gardens bring huge benefits to urban areas, filtering greenhouse gases, trapping dust particles, and helping to insulate the building, keeping rooms cool in summer and reducing the need for energy-guzzling air-conditioning.

JAMES WEBB SPACE TELESCOPE

LARGEST-EVER SPACE TELESCOPE

Launched on December 25, 2021, the James Webb Space Telescope is the largest space telescope ever. While its forerunner, the Hubble Space Telescope, is roughly the size of a school bus, the Webb is more like the size of a tennis court. It is so big that it had to be folded up inside a rocket for launching. It was not until January 8, 2022, that the telescope's mirror fully unfolded for use. Heading for a destination some 930,000 miles away from Earth, the Webb is about one hundred times more powerful than its predecessor. It is hoped that it will show astronomers parts of the universe never seen before, looking back in time to observe the earliest stars and galaxies.

1974 YEAR of discovery

36 NUMBER of years to create

8,000 TOTAL NUMBER of figures found

221–207 BCE
DURATION of the Ion Dynasty

FIRST EMPEROR OF CHINA

Emperor Qin Shi Huang was the first emperor of a unified China. Before his rule, the territory had been a collection of independent states. He was just forty-nine years old when he died.

QIN SHI HUANG'S TOMB

WORLD'S LARGEST TOMB OF A KNOWN INDIVIDUAL

Emperor Qin Shi Huang ruled China from 221 to 207 BCE. In 1974, people digging a well in the fields northeast of Xi'an, in the Shaanxi province, accidentally discovered the ancient tomb. Further investigation revealed a burial complex of over 20 square miles. A large pit contained 6,000 life-size terra-cotta warrior figures, each one different from the next and dressed according to rank. A second and third pit contained 2,000 more figures, clay horses, about 40,000 bronze weapons, and other artifacts. Historians think that 700,000 people worked for about thirty-six years to create this incredible mausoleum. The emperor's tomb remains sealed to preserve its contents and to protect workers from possible hazards, such as chemical poisoning from mercury in the surrounding soil.

WORLD'S LARGEST CASTLE
PRAGUE CASTLE

Founded in the late-ninth century CE, Prague Castle is the largest castle complex in the world. Covering an area of 750,000 square feet, the castle grounds span enough land for seven football fields, with buildings in various architectural styles that have been added and renovated during past centuries. Formerly the home of kings and emperors, the castle is now occupied by the president of the Czech Republic and his family and is also open to tourists. The palace contains four churches, including the famous St. Vitus Cathedral.

WORLD'S TALLEST SANDCASTLE

BLOKHUS SCULPTURE PARK
(DENMARK)

The record for the world's tallest sandcastle, standing at an impressive 69 feet, 5 inches tall, was set on July 2, 2021, in the Blokhus Sculpture Park, Denmark. Built in a bid to raise morale in the seaside town of Blokhus in the wake of the COVID-19 pandemic, the sandcastle is more than 10 feet taller than the previous record holder. It was created by Wilfred Stijger and a team of thirty sand sculptors and includes local sights and coastal sports among its decorative features. Right at the top is a sculpture of the virus that causes COVID-19 wearing a crown—a reminder of its control of the world over the last two years.

WORLD'S LONGEST LEGO® SHIP
WORLD DREAM

In 2018, 1,000 cruise passengers and volunteers came together to help build a replica of the *World Dream* cruise ship, a vessel owned by China's Dream Cruises Management Ltd. Boasting more than 2.5 million LEGO® blocks, this spectacle is the longest LEGO® ship ever built. It's a complete scaled-down replica of the *World Dream* cruise ship, with all eighteen of its decks, and measures 27 feet, 8.5 inches in length. Upon completion, it was placed in Hong Kong's Kai Tak Cruise Terminal for all to see.

WORLD'S LARGEST SCULPTURE CUT FROM A SINGLE PIECE OF STONE

SPHINX

The Great Sphinx stands guard near three large pyramids in Giza, Egypt. Historians believe ancient people created the sculpture about 4,500 years ago for the pharaoh Khafre. They carved the sphinx from one mass of limestone in the desert floor, creating a sculpture about 66 feet high and 240 feet long. It has the head of a pharaoh and the body of a lion. The sculpture may represent Ruti, a twin lion god from ancient myths that protected the sun god, Ra, and guarded entrances to the underworld. Sand has covered and preserved the Great Sphinx, but over many years, wind and humidity have worn parts of the soft limestone away, some of which have been restored using blocks of sand and quicklime.

GREAT SPHINX FACTS

Age: 4,500 years (estimated)

Length: 240 feet

Height: 66 feet

83

5 HIGH TECH

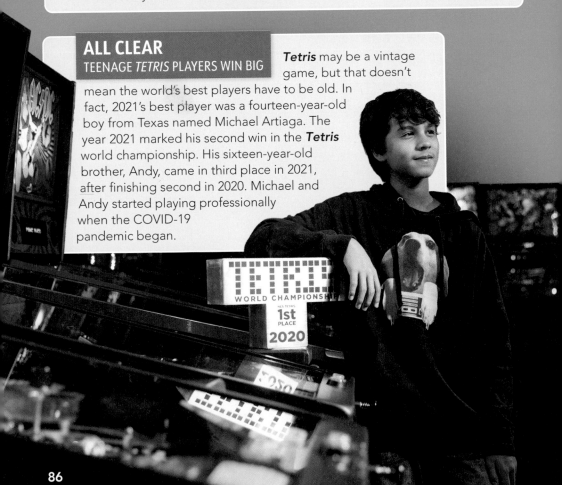

TRENDING

PULLING THE PLUG
WHEN FACEBOOK WENT DARK

Social media users got a shock in May 2021 when Facebook's apps experienced an unexpected shutdown. Instagram, WhatsApp, Facebook Messenger, and Facebook itself all went dark due to a server issue. Not only were users unable to post selfies or talk to friends, but businesses and organizations relying on the apps found it impossible to function—and Facebook's own employees were unable to access their offices or communications platforms, which are run on Facebook servers. The outage took nearly seven hours to resolve, and rumor has it engineers had to manually switch the servers back on!

ALL CLEAR
TEENAGE *TETRIS* PLAYERS WIN BIG

Tetris may be a vintage game, but that doesn't mean the world's best players have to be old. In fact, 2021's best player was a fourteen-year-old boy from Texas named Michael Artiaga. The year 2021 marked his second win in the *Tetris* world championship. His sixteen-year-old brother, Andy, came in third place in 2021, after finishing second in 2020. Michael and Andy started playing professionally when the COVID-19 pandemic began.

COPY AND PASTE
GENETICALLY EDITED PRODUCE GOES TO MARKET

The future is here! The first food modified by Nobel Prize–winning CRISPR genome-editing technology was sold in Japan in 2021. Sanatech Seed's Sicilian Rouge High GABA tomato was edited to contain up to five times the normal amount of gamma-aminobutyric acid (GABA), which is useful in lowering people's blood pressure. Sanatech Seed started selling the tomatoes in September and is hopeful that the acceptance of the tomatoes is just the beginning for gene editing.

YOUNG ENTREPRENEUR
WEIRD WHALES EARN BIG

In 2021, twelve-year-old Benyamin Ahmed made the equivalent of over $400,000 in the cryptocurrency Ethereum, selling Python-generated images called "Weird Whales" as non-fungible tokens (NFTs). All 3,350 of his whales sold out in less than a day. NFTs, which went big during the pandemic, are controversial due to their huge environmental impact—just one NFT transaction is believed to have a carbon emission footprint of about 106 pounds of CO_2.

NO LEGS? NO PROBLEM!
JUMPING ROBOT MAKES ITS DEBUT

A tiny new robot critter was announced in *Nature Communications* journal in December 2021, impressing readers with its skills in "rapid, continuous, and steered jumping" despite having no legs. Designed by Chongqing University's Rui Chen and his team, the 2.5-inch-long robot is shaped like a pancake and can jump up to six times its body length per second and close to eight times its height!

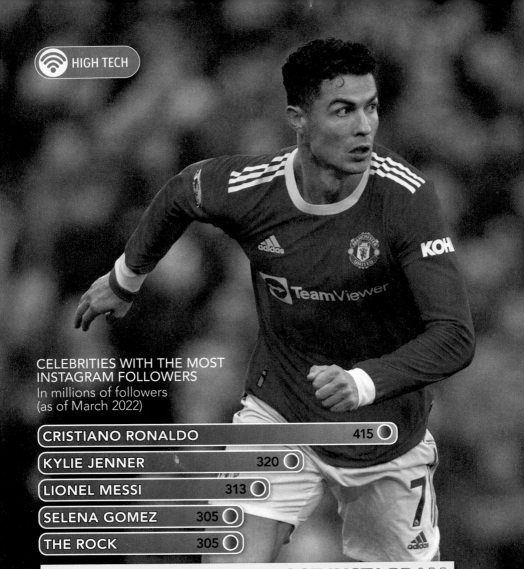

CELEBRITIES WITH THE MOST INSTAGRAM FOLLOWERS

In millions of followers
(as of March 2022)

CRISTIANO RONALDO	415
KYLIE JENNER	320
LIONEL MESSI	313
SELENA GOMEZ	305
THE ROCK	305

CELEBRITY WITH THE MOST INSTAGRAM FOLLOWERS
CRISTIANO RONALDO

Portuguese soccer icon Cristiano Ronaldo was once again the year's most-followed celebrity on Instagram in 2022. He now has 415 million followers, a staggering increase of 144 million over last year's figure. Argentine soccer hero Lionel Messi also made it into the top five, with 313 million followers. In 2021, Ronaldo delighted fans of the UK's Manchester United when he signed up for a second spell wearing the team's world-famous red-and-white shirt. The star was just eighteen years old when he first signed for the "Red Devils" in 2003.

MOST RETWEETED TWEET EVER
YUSAKU MAEZAWA

↻ 4.4m   ⌷ Share this Tweet

Yusaku Maezawa holds the title for most retweeted tweet of all time, with a whopping 4.4 million retweets. Celebrating his company's high Christmas–New Year earnings in 2018–2019, the Japanese billionaire posted a tweet with accompanying images promising to split one hundred million yen ($937,638) among one hundred randomly chosen people. Another giveaway from Yusaku (who tweets as @yousuck2020) also made the list as the second-most retweeted tweet. The prospect of free money definitely helped motivate people to make this one go viral!

MOST-DOWNLOADED GAME APP

SUBWAY SURFERS

After three consecutive years in the no. 2 spot, *Subway Surfers* finally made it back to the top of the leaderboard in 2021 for most-downloaded game app across the globe. Launched over a decade ago, in May 2012, the endless running game sees you collecting coins while dodging trams, trains, and other moving obstacles, with a security guard hot on your tail. A perennial favorite, the game amassed 191 million downloads. Meanwhile, last year's no. 1, *Among Us*, slipped all the way down to no. 5, with 152 million downloads.

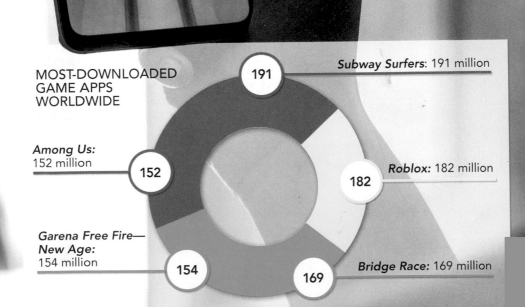

MOST-DOWNLOADED GAME APPS WORLDWIDE

Subway Surfers: 191 million

Among Us: 152 million

Roblox: 182 million

Garena Free Fire— New Age: 154 million

Bridge Race: 169 million

MOST-VIEWED YOUTUBE VIDEO EVER
"BABY SHARK DANCE"

More than half of the top 10 most-viewed YouTube videos now are specifically for entertaining children, and the no. 1 spot is no exception. The addictive "Baby Shark Dance" video by South Korean brand Pinkfong (by SmartStudy) has been viewed at least 10.6 billion times since its upload in June 2016. The simple song and its accompanying dance moves went viral in 2018, and "Baby Shark Dance" now has its own line of merchandise as well as an animated series on Nickelodeon. There is even a remix starring Luis Fonsi, which is ironic, given that Fonsi's "Despacito" was no. 1 prior to "Baby Shark Dance."

MOST POPULAR EMOJI

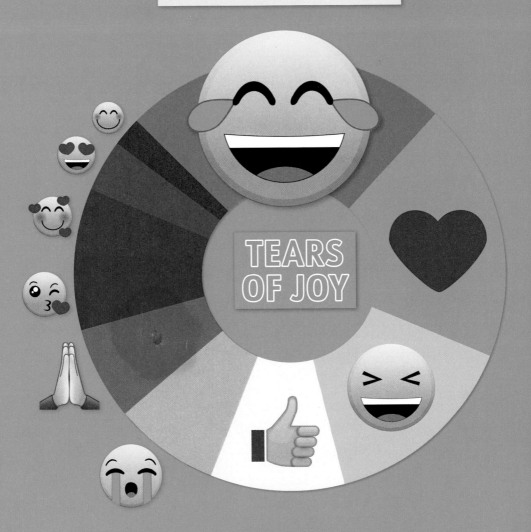

TEARS OF JOY

Despite being deemed hopelessly uncool by Gen Z, Tears of Joy claimed the top spot as the most popular emoji in 2021. Representing an incredible share of more than 5 percent of ALL emoji usage, this is the second time this emoji has come out on top. There are more than 3,500 emojis currently in existence, and yet the top 100 make up about 82 percent of usage. Leading emojis in other categories include the Crown (clothing), the Flexed Biceps (body parts), and the Butterfly (animals).

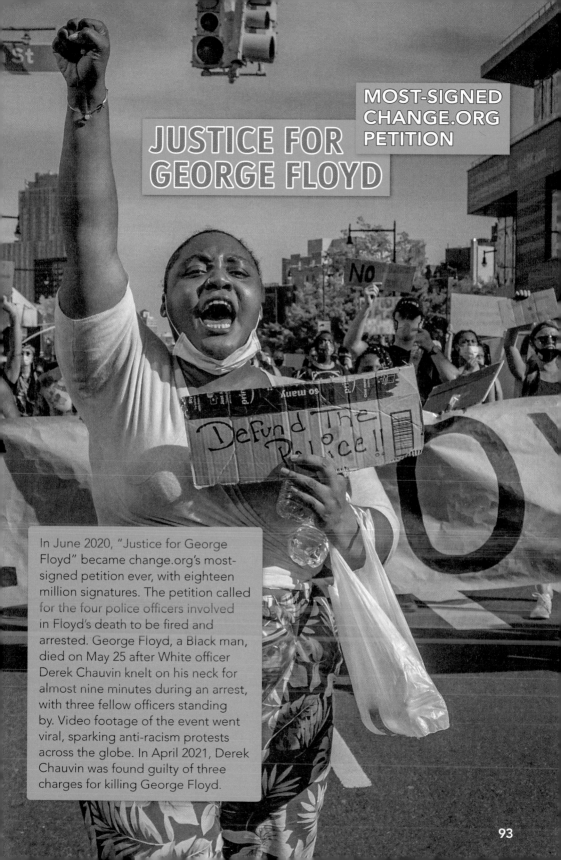

JUSTICE FOR GEORGE FLOYD

MOST-SIGNED CHANGE.ORG PETITION

In June 2020, "Justice for George Floyd" became change.org's most-signed petition ever, with eighteen million signatures. The petition called for the four police officers involved in Floyd's death to be fired and arrested. George Floyd, a Black man, died on May 25 after White officer Derek Chauvin knelt on his neck for almost nine minutes during an arrest, with three fellow officers standing by. Video footage of the event went viral, sparking anti-racism protests across the globe. In April 2021, Derek Chauvin was found guilty of three charges for killing George Floyd.

MOST-VIEWED VIDEO ON TIKTOK

ZACH KING

Proving that the world still loves watching magic, four of the five most-viewed videos on the TikTok platform as of August 2021 come from American illusionist Zach King. The most popular TikTok video ever, with 2.2 billion views, shows King pulling off a Harry Potter–based trick in which he uses a longboard and mirrored surface to create the illusion of flying on a broomstick down a California street. The only TikTok in the top five that is not by King comes from makeup YouTuber James Charles, whose "Sisters Christmas Party" 2019 TikTok became the app's second-most viewed ever with 1.7 billion views.

CHARLI D'AMELIO

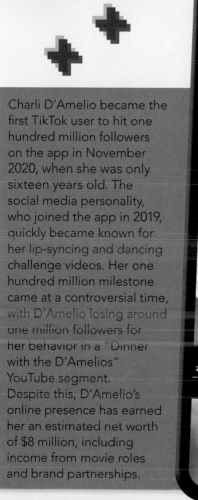

Charli D'Amelio became the first TikTok user to hit one hundred million followers on the app in November 2020, when she was only sixteen years old. The social media personality, who joined the app in 2019, quickly became known for her lip-syncing and dancing challenge videos. Her one hundred million milestone came at a controversial time, with D'Amelio losing around one million followers for her behavior in a "Dinner with the D'Amelios" YouTube segment. Despite this, D'Amelio's online presence has earned her an estimated net worth of $8 million, including income from movie roles and brand partnerships.

👤 10.4M

DOG WITH THE MOST INSTAGRAM FOLLOWERS

JIFFPOM

On May 3, 2017, and with 4.8 million followers, Jiffpom broke the Guinness World Record for being the most popular dog on Instagram. Three years later, in June 2020, the dog's follower count was at the 10.4-million mark. Jiffpom's owner posts snapshots of the fluffy little dog dressed in cute outfits, and Jiffpom even has a website. The Pomeranian from the United States has other records to boast of, too. At one time, he held the record for fastest dog to cover a distance of 16.4 feet on his front legs (7.76 seconds). Another time, he was the record holder for covering 32.8 feet on his hind legs (6.56 seconds).

CAT WITH THE MOST INSTAGRAM FOLLOWERS

NALA CAT

In January 2020, and with a total of 4.3 million followers, Nala Cat broke the Guinness World Record for cat with the most followers on Instagram. By June 2020, the popular feline's record had risen to 4.4 million. Adopted from a shelter at just five months old, the Siamese-Tabby charms online viewers around the world with her bright blue eyes and supercute headgear.

4.4M

BEST-SELLING VIDEO GAME EVER

TETRIS

Tetris, developed by Russian computer scientist Alexey Pajitnov in 1984, has sold over 500 million copies worldwide—more than any other game. It has been available on almost every video game console since its creation and has seen a resurgence in sales as an app for cell phones and tablets. The iconic puzzle game was the first video game to be exported from the Soviet Union to the United States, the first to be played in outer space, and is often listed as one of the best video games of all time. In 2019, Nintendo released *Tetris 99* for Nintendo Switch—a multiplayer version of the game that sees ninety-nine players compete online.

CALL OF DUTY
BLACK OPS COLD WAR

Released in November 2020, **Call of Duty: Black Ops Cold War** quickly made history as one of the country's top-selling games, hitting the top 20 all-time list with only a couple months of sales. The game made $678 million in its first six weeks. It went on to top the charts again in 2021, despite the much-anticipated release of **Call of Duty: Vanguard**. **Call of Duty** has generated $27 billion since its inception in 2003, according to Activision. The entire gaming industry saw a boost from the onset of the COVID-19 pandemic, with people having more time indoors adding up to more money spent on games.

BEST-SELLING PS2
CONSOLE OF ALL TIME

PlayStation's legendary console, the PS2, is still the best-selling console of all time, with parent company Sony confirming the sale of more than 158 million units. Launched in 2000, the PS2 was particularly successful because it could play PS2 games, PS1 games, and even DVDs. More modern consoles have struggled to match the PS2's success; in fact, the majority of the top 10 best-selling consoles are more than a decade old. In second place, with around 155 million units sold, is the Nintendo DS, released in 2004, and in third place is 1989's classic Game Boy, which sold 118.69 million units before it was discontinued fourteen years later.

BEST-SELLING VIDEO GAME FRANCHISE OF ALL TIME

MARIO

Nintendo's **Mario** franchise has sold 681 million units since the first game was released in 1981. Since then, Mario, his brother Luigi, and other characters like Princess Peach and Yoshi have become household names, starring in a number of games. In the early games, like **Super Mario World**, players jump over obstacles, collect tokens, and capture flags as Mario journeys through the Mushroom Kingdom to save the princess. The franchise has since diversified to include other popular games, such as **Mario Kart**, a racing game showcasing the inhabitants and landscapes of the Mushroom Kingdom.

BEST-SELLING VIDEO GAME FRANCHISES
Units sold in millions

- **Mario** (Nintendo)
- **Tetris** (The Tetris Company)
- **Call of Duty** (Activision)
- **Pokémon** (Game Freak)
- **Grand Theft Auto** (Rockstar North)

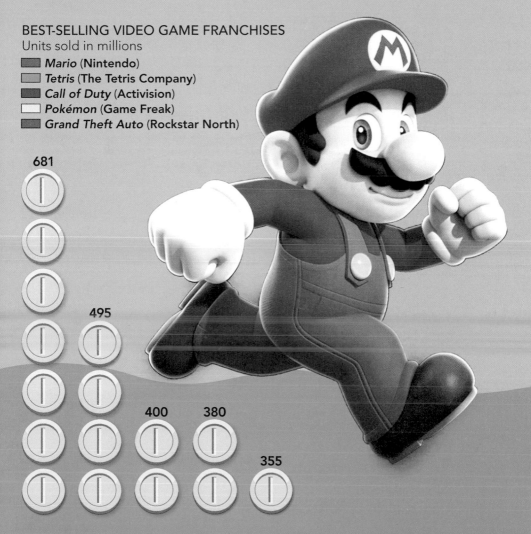

681

495

400   380

355

BIGGEST CONVENTION FOR A SINGLE VIDEO GAME

MINEFAIRE 2016

According to Guinness World Records, Minefaire 2016, a gathering of **Minecraft** fans, was the biggest convention ever for a single video game. Held October 15–16 at the Greater Philadelphia Expo Center in Oaks, Pennsylvania, the event attracted 12,140 people. Game developer Markus Persson created **Minecraft** in 2009 and sold it to Microsoft in 2014 for $2.5 billion. Gamers can play alone or with other players online. The game involves breaking and placing blocks to build whatever gamers can imagine—from simple constructions to huge virtual worlds. Attendance was not the only element of Minefaire to gain world-record status. On October 15, the largest-ever **Minecraft** architecture lesson attracted 342 attendees, and American gamer Lestat Wade broke the record for building the tallest staircase in **Minecraft** in one minute.

MINEFAIRE STATS:

12,140 Number of people attending Minefaire

150,000 Total area, in square feet, of Minecraft-centered attractions

3 Number of Guinness World Records broken at the fair

TOP-EARNING YOUTUBER
MRBEAST

Jimmy Donaldson, better known as MrBeast, is famed for his outlandish and generous YouTube giveaways—$10,000 to sit in a bathtub of snakes, anyone?—so it should surprise nobody that he's also raking in the cash. In 2021, his $54 million in earnings made him the highest-grossing YouTuber of all time. He also made a bold foray into the food industry, creating the "MrBeast Burger" virtual restaurant brand, which partners with existing restaurants around the United States to make and deliver his menu.

WORLD'S SMALLEST SURGICAL ROBOT

VERSIUS

British robot specialists Cambridge Medical Robotics developed the world's smallest surgical robot in 2017. Operated by a surgeon using a console guide with a 3-D screen, the robot is able to carry out keyhole surgery. The scientists modeled the robot, called Versius, on the human arm, giving it similar wrist joints to allow maximum flexibility. Keyhole surgery involves making very small cuts on the surface of a person's body, through which a surgeon can then operate. The recovery time of the patient is usually quicker when operated on in this way.

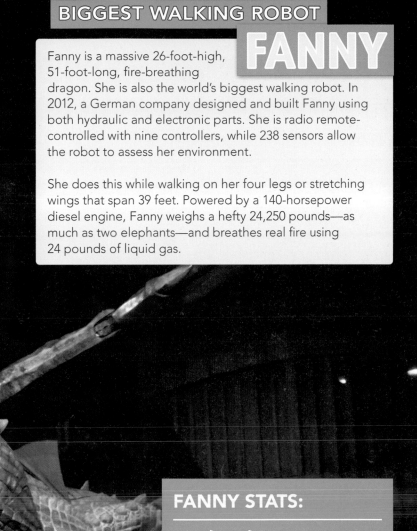

BIGGEST WALKING ROBOT

FANNY

Fanny is a massive 26-foot-high, 51-foot-long, fire-breathing dragon. She is also the world's biggest walking robot. In 2012, a German company designed and built Fanny using both hydraulic and electronic parts. She is radio remote-controlled with nine controllers, while 238 sensors allow the robot to assess her environment.

She does this while walking on her four legs or stretching wings that span 39 feet. Powered by a 140-horsepower diesel engine, Fanny weighs a hefty 24,250 pounds—as much as two elephants—and breathes real fire using 24 pounds of liquid gas.

FANNY STATS:

09/27/2012 Date of Fanny's launch

26´ 10˝ Fanny's height in feet and inches

51´ 6˝ Fanny's length in feet and inches

12´ Fanny's body width in feet

39´ Fanny's wingspan in feet

TRENDING

NOT JUST FOR HUMANS
COVID SPREADS TO BIG CATS

While the human population was taking lateral flow tests, lions and tigers in Washington, DC, were also getting tested for COVID-19. After the big cats at the Smithsonian National Zoo began coughing and sneezing, acting tired, and losing weight, their keepers tested them for the virus. Six African lions, a Sumatran tiger, and two Amur tigers tested positive for COVID-19 in September 2021 and had to receive treatment. Thankfully, all nine recovered, and staff rolled out a special version of the vaccine to other at-risk zoo animals.

AN EERIE OPENING
EMPTY STANDS AT TOKYO OLYMPICS

It was inevitable that the pandemic would take its toll on 2021's Tokyo Olympics, but its opening ceremony made waves as people watching around the world witnessed the celebrations take place in a mostly empty arena. Less than 1,000 spectators watched in person in an arena that holds 68,000. The ceremony saw protests from people calling for the games to be canceled, and it was paused for a minute's silence for those who died during the pandemic.

SWEET INCENTIVE
FREE DOUGHNUTS FOR THE VACCINATED

World governments encouraged people to get vaccinated against COVID-19, some of them using creative campaigns. Doughnut legend Krispy Kreme took the cake with their sweet offer of a free doughnut for anyone with a stamped vaccination card. They then proceeded to outdo themselves August 30–September 5, 2021, when they upped it to two doughnuts.

1 MILLION
OMICRON WREAKS HAVOC

On January 10, 2022, the United States broke global records, reporting an incredible 1.35 million new daily cases of COVID-19. The dramatic spike in new cases was an all-time high due to the highly contagious Omicron variant, which hit the nation hard and was responsible for the majority of these new cases.

ZOO-MAZING
MOST SURPRISING VACCINATION SITE

Belgian children had a unique vaccination experience in early 2022, when Antwerp Zoo set up a vaccination center for kids between the ages of five and eleven. Children were distracted with laser pointers during the jab, and once it was done, they were allowed to explore the zoo's conservatory. Such ideas might explain why Flanders, the region where Antwerp is located, vaccinated children at a rate three times higher than the rest of Belgium. By February 2022, around 45 percent of five- to eleven-year-olds in Flanders had been vaccinated.

AMAZING ANIMALS

TRENDING

Giant pandas Mei Xiang and Tian Tian stole the nation's hearts in February 2021 when a camera feed of the two of them playing in the snow at the National Zoo in Washington, DC, went viral. The pair's cub, Xiao Qi Ji, followed in their footsteps a year later, with the zoo releasing a video of the adorable little panda tumbling in the snow in early 2022.

SNOW DAY
PANDA PLAY AT THE NATIONAL ZOO

A HUGE DISCOVERY
LARGEST FLYING CREATURE

New research published in 2021 told us more about the pterosaur *Quetzalcoatlus*. With an amazing 40-foot wingspan, it is thought to be the largest flying creature ever to have lived! US paleontologists Matthew Brown and Kevin Padian led a team in reconstructing a *Quetzalcoatlus* from bones found at Big Bend National Park, Texas, and then worked together with a biomechanical and an aerospace engineer to figure out how it might fly.

UNLIKELY FRIENDS
OCTOPUS DOCUMENTARY GOES VIRAL

A nature documentary became an unexpected hit in 2020 as Netflix viewers went wild for *My Octopus Teacher*. The film follows Craig Foster, a South African conservationist, who began diving in frozen kelp forests every day—without a wet suit or scuba gear—and befriended an octopus, following it and filming it underwater for a whole year of its life.

TAKING OVER
AN ABUNDANCE OF MICE

As if a pandemic wasn't enough, Eastern Australia spent the first half of 2021 gripped by a mice plague. Beginning with the harvest season of 2020, the mouse population rose so dramatically that homes, schools, hospitals, and other buildings became overrun. Wellington's prison even had to be evacuated due to concerns about the health of the inmates. The mice caused so much damage to farmers' crops that the Australian government committed AU$150 million (about US$106 million) to help deal with the problem.

WALRUS DETECTIVES
ENLISTING VOLUNTEERS FOR CENSUS DATA

In 2021, the World Wildlife Fund (WWF) and British Antarctic Survey's "Walrus from Space" initiative asked people to become "walrus detectives," spotting them in satellite images taken from space. Walruses, who rely on sea ice, are at risk due to climate change, so it is important to count all of them. Anyone with half an hour and a computer or laptop is encouraged to join in on the five-year project.

WORLD'S SLEEPIEST ANIMAL KOALA

Australia's koala sleeps for up to twenty hours a day and still manages to look sleepy when awake. This is due to the koala's unbelievably monotonous diet. It feeds, mostly at night, on the aromatic leaves of eucalyptus trees. The leaves have little nutritional or calorific value, so the marsupial saves energy by snoozing. It jams its rear end into a fork in the branches of its favorite tree so it cannot fall out while asleep.

WORLD'S BEST GLIDER
FLYING SQUIRREL

Flying squirrels are champion animal gliders. The Japanese giant flying squirrel has been scientifically recorded making flights over distances of up to 164 feet from tree to tree. These creatures have been estimated to make 656-foot flights when flying downhill. The squirrel remains aloft using a special flap of skin on either side of its body, which stretches between wrist and ankle. Its fluffy tail acts as a stabilizer to keep it steady, and the squirrel changes direction by twisting its wrists and moving its limbs.

WORLD'S GLIDERS
Distance in feet

- Flying squirrel
- Flying fish
- Colugo, or flying lemur
- Draco, or flying lizard
- Flying squid

| 164 | 197 | 230 | 655 | 656 |

WORLD'S HEAVIEST LAND MAMMAL
AFRICAN BUSH ELEPHANT

The African bush elephant is the world's largest living land animal. The biggest known bush elephant stood 13.8 feet at the shoulder and had an estimated weight of 13.5 tons. The African bush elephant is also the animal with the largest outer ears. The outsize flappers help keep the animal cool on the open savanna. The Asian elephant has much smaller earflaps, because it lives in the forest and is not exposed to the same high temperatures.

WORLD'S TINIEST BAT
KITTI'S HOG-NOSED BAT

This little critter, the Kitti's hog-nosed bat, is just 1.3 inches long, with a wingspan of 6.7 inches, and weighs 0.07–0.10 ounces. It's tied for first place as the world's smallest mammal with Savi's Etruscan shrew, which is longer at 2.1 inches but lighter at 0.04–0.06 ounces. The bat lives in west central Thailand and southeast Myanmar, and the shrew is found in areas from the Mediterranean to Southeast Asia.

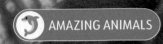

WORLD'S LARGEST PRIMATE
GORILLA

The largest living primates on Earth are the eastern gorillas, and the biggest subspecies among them is the very rare mountain gorilla. The tallest known was an adult male silverback, named for the color of the fur on his back. He stood at 6.4 feet tall, but he was an exception—silverbacks generally grow no bigger than 5.9 feet tall. Gorillas have long arms. The record holder had an arm span measuring 8.9 feet, while adult male humans have an average arm span of just 5.9 feet.

MANDRILL

The male mandrill's face is as flamboyant as his rear end. The vivid colors of both are brightest at breeding time. The colors announce to his rivals that he is an alpha male and he has the right to breed with the females. His exceptionally long and fanglike canine teeth reinforce his dominance. The mandrill is the world's largest monkey, as well as the most colorful.

FASTEST LAND ANIMALS
Top speed

Cheetah	61 mph
Ostrich	60 mph
Pronghorn	55 mph
Springbok	55 mph
Lion	30 mph

WORLD'S FASTEST LAND ANIMAL
CHEETAH

The fastest reliably recorded running speed of any animal was that of a zoo-bred cheetah that reached an incredible 61 miles per hour on a flat surface. The record was achieved in 2012, from a standing start by a captive cheetah at Cincinnati Zoo. More recently, wild cheetahs have been timed while actually hunting their prey in the bush in Botswana. Using GPS technology and special tracking collars, the scientists found that these cheetahs had a top speed of 58 miles per hour over rough terrain.

DRACULA ANT

The Dracula ant, **Mystrium camillae**, of tropical areas of Africa, Southeast Asia, and Australasia, makes the fastest movement of any known animal on Earth. In the time it takes you to blink, it can open and close its jaws *five thousand* times. It does this by pressing its jaws together, storing energy like a spring, and then sliding them past each other at up to 200 miles per hour. Such fast jaws allow the ant to stun or kill its prey, such as fast-moving centipedes, which have their own formidable jaws!

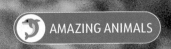

WORLD'S LARGEST BIG CAT
TIGER

There are only five big cats that roam Earth: tiger, lion, jaguar, leopard, and snow leopard. The biggest and heaviest is the Siberian, or Amur, tiger, which lives in the taiga (boreal forest) of eastern Siberia, where it hunts deer and wild boar. The largest reliably measured tigers have been about 11.8 feet long and weighed 705 pounds, but there have been claims for larger individuals, such as the male shot in the Sikhote-Alin Mountains in 1950. That tiger weighed 847 pounds.

HOWLER MONKEY

The howler monkeys of Latin America are deafening. Males have an especially large hyoid bone. This horseshoe-shaped bone in the neck creates a chamber that makes the monkey's deep guttural growls sound louder for longer. It is said that their calls can be heard up to 3 miles away. Both males and females call, and they holler mainly in the morning. It is thought that these calls are often one troop of monkeys telling neighboring troops where they are.

GIRAFFE

Giraffes living on the savannas of eastern and southern Africa are the world's tallest animals. The tallest known bull giraffe measured 19 feet from the ground to the top of his horns. He could have looked over the top of a London double-decker bus or peered into the upstairs window of a two-story house. Despite having considerably longer necks than we do, giraffes have the same number of neck vertebrae. They also have long legs, with which they can either speedily escape from predators or kick them to keep them away.

REACHING GREAT HEIGHTS

A giraffe's tongue can grow up to 21 inches in length. This helps the animal reach leaves on the topmost branches of a tree when it is looking for food.

GIRAFFE STATS

6 HEIGHT OF A CALF AT BIRTH IN FEET

25 AVERAGE LIFE SPAN IN YEARS

100 ADULT'S DAILY FOOD CONSUMPTION IN POUNDS OF LEAVES AND TWIGS

WORLD'S LONGEST TOOTH

NARWHAL

The narwhal's "sword" is an enormously elongated spiral tooth, or tusk. In male narwhals it can grow to more than 8.2 feet long. Only about 15 percent of females grow a tusk, which typically is smaller than a male tusk, with a less noticeable spiral. It has been suggested that the tusk serves as an adornment to attract the opposite sex—the larger a male narwhal's tusk, the more attractive he is to females. It is also thought to be a sensory organ that detects changes in the seawater, such as saltiness, which could help the narwhal find food. Observers have also noted that the narwhal uses its tusk to stun prey.

THE WORLD'S LARGEST LIVING ANIMAL
BLUE WHALE

Blue whales are truly colossal. The largest one accurately measured was 110 feet long, and the heaviest weighed 209 tons. They feed on tiny krill, which they filter from the sea. On land, the largest known animal was a Titanosaur—a huge dinosaur that lived 101 million years ago in what is now Argentina. A skeleton found in 2014 suggests the creature was 121 feet long and weighed 77 tons. It belongs to a young Titanosaur, so an adult may have been bigger than a blue whale.

WORLD'S BIGGEST FISH
WHALE SHARK

Recognizable from its spotted skin and enormous size, the whale shark is the world's largest living fish. It grows to a maximum length of about 66 feet. Like the blue whale, this fish feeds on some of the smallest creatures: krill, marine larvae, small fish, and fish eggs. The whale shark is also a great traveler. One female was tracked swimming 4,800 miles from Mexico—where hundreds of whale sharks gather each summer to feed—to the middle of the South Atlantic Ocean, where it is thought she may have given birth.

THE SHARK MOST DANGEROUS TO PEOPLE
GREAT WHITE SHARK

SHARK ATTACKS
Number of humans attacked

- Great white shark
- Tiger shark
- Bull shark
- Blacktip shark

354	138	121	41

The great white shark is at the top of the list for the highest number of attacks on people. The largest reliably measured fish was 21 feet long, making it the largest predatory fish in the sea. Its jaws are lined with large, triangular, serrated teeth that can slice through flesh, sinew, and even bone. However, there were just seventy-three reported unprovoked attacks by sharks of any kind in 2021, and nine of those proved fatal. Humans are not this creature's top food of choice. People don't have enough fat on their bodies. Mature white sharks prefer blubber-rich seals, dolphins, and whales. It is likely that many of the attacks on people are probably cases of mistaken identity.

WORLD'S LARGEST LIZARD
KOMODO DRAGON

There are dragons on Indonesia's Komodo Island, and they're dangerous. The Komodo dragon's jaws are lined with sixty replaceable, serrated, backward-pointing teeth. Its saliva is laced with deadly bacteria and venom that the dragon works into a wound, ensuring its prey will die quickly. Prey can be as big as a pig or deer, because this lizard is the world's largest. It can grow up to 10.3 feet long and weigh 366 pounds.

WORLD'S DEADLIEST FROG
POISON DART FROG

A poison dart frog's skin exudes toxins. There are several species, and the more vivid a frog's color, the more deadly its poison. The skin color warns potential predators that the frogs are not good to eat, although one snake is immune to the chemicals and happily feeds on these creatures. It is thought that the frogs do not manufacture their own poisons, but obtain the chemicals from their diet of ants, millipedes, and mites. The most deadly species to people is also the largest, Colombia's golden poison dart frog. At just one inch long, a single frog has enough poison to kill ten to twenty people.

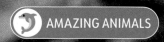
WORLD'S LARGEST REPTILE

SALTWATER CROCODILE

The saltwater crocodile, or "saltie," is the world's largest living reptile. Males can grow to over 20 feet long, but a few old-timers become real monsters. A well-known crocodile in the Segama River, Borneo, left an impression on a sandbank that measured 33 feet. The saltie can be found in areas from eastern India to northeast Australia, where it lives in mangroves, estuaries, and rivers. It is sometimes found out at sea. The saltie is an ambush predator, grabbing any animal that enters its domain—including people. Saltwater crocodiles account for twenty to thirty attacks on people per year, up to half of which are fatal.

NANO-CHAMELEON

In a mountain forest in northern Madagascar lives the smallest known reptile in the world: the nano-chameleon *Brookesia nana*. From his snout to the tip of his tail, the male of the species is just 0.85 inches long—that's roughly the length of a sunflower seed. The female is a little longer: 1.14 inches. They live among the leaf litter on the forest floor, where they hunt for mites and springtails. They are well camouflaged with a light brown and gray body, and they hide from predators among blades of grass. Unlike most chameleons, they do not change color, but they do have the chameleon's exceptionally long, extendable tongue to capture prey.

133

WORLD'S SMELLIEST BIRD
HOATZIN

The hoatzin eats leaves, flowers, and fruit. It ferments the food in its crop (a pouch in its esophagus). This habit leaves the bird with a foul odor, which has led people to nickname the hoatzin the "stinkbird." About the size of a pheasant, this bird lives in the Amazon and Orinoco river basins of South America. A hoatzin chick has sharp claws on its wings, like a pterodactyl. If threatened by a snake, the chick jumps from the nest into the water, then uses its wing claws to help it climb back up.

RIBBON-TAILED ASTRAPIA

The ribbon-tailed astrapia has the longest feathers in relation to body size of any wild bird. The male, which has a beautiful, iridescent blue-green head, sports a pair of white ribbon-shaped tail feathers that are more than 3.3 feet long—three times the length of its 13-inch-long body. It is one of Papua New Guinea's birds of paradise and lives in the mountain forests of central New Guinea, where males sometimes have to untangle their tails from the foliage before they can fly.

THE WORLD'S LARGEST NESTS
Diameter in inches

- Bald eagle
- White stork
- Golden eagle

114

57

55

BIRD THAT BUILDS LARGEST NEST
BALD EAGLE

With a wingspan over 6.6 feet, bald eagles need space to land and take off—so their nests can be gargantuan. Over the years, a nest built by a pair of bald eagles in St. Petersburg, Florida, has taken on epic proportions. Measuring 9.5 feet across and 20 feet deep, it is made of sticks, grass, and moss. At one stage it was thought to have weighed at least 2 tons, making it the largest nest ever constructed by a pair of birds. Although one pair nests at a time, these huge structures are often the work of several pairs of birds, each building on top of the work of their predecessors.

WORLD'S LARGEST BIRD EGG
AFRICAN OSTRICH EGG

The African ostrich lays the largest eggs of any living bird, yet they are the smallest eggs relative to the size of the mother's body. Each egg is some 5.9 inches long and weighs about 3.5–5 pounds, while the mother is about 6.2 feet tall and the male is about 7.8 feet tall, making the ostrich the world's largest living bird. The female lays about fifty eggs per year, and each egg contains as much yolk and albumen as twenty-four hens' eggs. It takes an hour to soft-boil an ostrich egg!

EMPEROR PENGUIN STATS

80 AVERAGE WEIGHT OF AN ADULT IN POUNDS

1,640 DEPTH AN ADULT CAN SWIM TO IN FEET

22 LENGTH OF TIME UNDERWATER IN MINUTES

At 4 feet tall, the emperor penguin is the world's biggest living penguin. It has a most curious lifestyle, breeding during the long, dark Antarctic winter. The female lays a single egg and carefully passes it to the male. She then heads out to sea to feed, while he remains with the egg balanced on his feet and tucked under a fold of blubber-rich skin. There he stands with all the other penguin dads, huddled together to keep warm in the blizzards and 100-mile-per-hour winds that scour the icy continent. Come spring, the egg hatches, the female returns, and Mom and Dad swap duties, taking turns to feed and care for their fluffy chick.

EMPEROR PENGUIN

FIVE OF THE WORLD'S PENGUINS
Height in inches

- Emperor
- King
- Gentoo
- Macaroni
- Galápagos

19 28 35 39 48

FOUR OF THE WORLD'S SPIDERS
Leg span in inches

- Giant huntsman spider
- Goliath bird-eating tarantula
- Brazilian wandering spider
- Golden silk orb-weaver

12   12

11   11

5.9   5.9

5   5

GOLIATH BIRD-EATING TARANTULA WORLD'S HEAVIEST SPIDER

The size of a dinner plate, the female goliath bird-eating tarantula has a leg span of 11 inches and weighs up to 6.17 ounces. This is the world's heaviest spider and a real nightmare for an arachnophobe (someone with a fear of spiders). Its fangs can pierce a person's skin, but its venom is no worse than a beesting. The hairs on its body are more of a hazard. When threatened, it rubs its abdomen with its hind legs and releases tiny hairs that cause severe irritation to the skin. Despite its name, this spider does not actually eat birds very often.

DESERT LOCUST

Flying insects are difficult to clock, and many impressive speeds have been claimed over the years. The fastest airspeed reliably timed was by fifteen desert locusts that managed an average of 21 miles per hour. Airspeed is the actual speed at which the insect flies. It is different from ground speed, which is often enhanced by favorable winds. A black cutworm moth whizzed along at 70 miles per hour while riding the winds ahead of a cold front. The most shocking measurement, however, is that of a horsefly with an estimated airspeed of 90 miles per hour while chasing an air-gun pellet! Understandably, this is one speed that has not been verified!

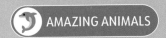
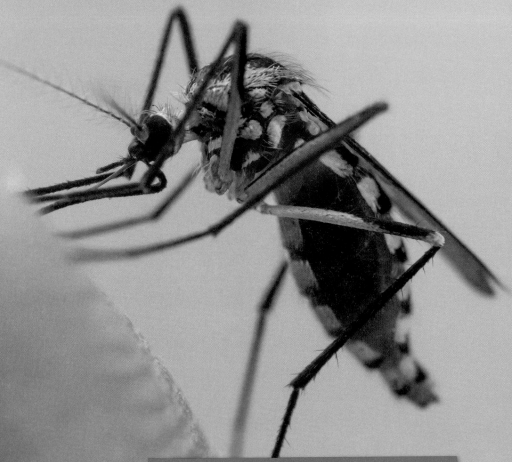

WORLD'S DEADLIEST ANIMAL
MOSQUITO

Female mosquitoes live on the blood of birds and mammals—humans included. However, the problem is not what they take, but what they leave behind. In some mosquitoes' saliva are organisms that cause the world's most deadly illnesses, including malaria, yellow fever, dengue fever, West Nile virus, and encephalitis. It is estimated that mosquitoes transmit diseases to 700 million people every year, of which 725,000 die. In 2021, the World Health Organization (WHO) announced the release of a vaccine that can help prevent a mosquito-borne disease called malaria, and that has the potential to save tens of thousands of lives.

WORLD'S LONGEST INSECT MIGRATION
GLOBE SKIMMER

Each year millions of dragonflies fly thousands of miles across the Indian Ocean from South India to East Africa. Most of them are globe skimmers, a species known to fly long distances and at altitudes up to 3,280 feet. They can travel 2,175 miles in 24 hours. Coral cays on the way have little open fresh water, so the insects stay there for a few days before moving on to East Africa. Here, they follow the rains, at each stop taking advantage of temporary rainwater pools to lay their eggs to hatch where their young can rapidly develop. Four generations are involved in a round trip of about 11,000 miles—farther than the distance from New York to Sydney.

TRENDING

ANYTHING IS PAWS-IBLE!
MIA'S OBSTACLE COURSE GOES VIRAL

One of the most popular animal videos on TikTok in 2021 saw Mia, "Ambassador of Fluff," testing her mettle against a homemade obstacle course. Viewers watched in delight as the stealth sensation hopped over barriers made of plastic cups at the cat's home in Salford, England. While the obstacle course was designed to keep Mia fit, it seems to have provided hours of fun! With more than 184 million views, Mia's was the most watched TikTok in the UK.

POOCH PIONEER
SHOW WINNER RAISES AWARENESS

When Wasabi claimed top prize at New York's Westminster Dog Show, he sparked a social media debate about dog breeding practices. The Pekingese is bred to enhance its cute characteristics, often at the cost of its health. Its flat face has become even flatter, for example, causing breathing problems. Wasabi is well cared for by his owners, but his victory has raised an important issue in the world of dog breeding and showing.

BONES DAY
NOODLE THE PUG SETS THE MOOD

Thirteen-year-old Noodle's efforts to get up for his daily walk became an internet sensation in 2021. Each morning, owner Jonathan Graziano puts the pug in a standing position and sees if he'll stay standing or flop back down on his bed. If he doesn't stand, it's a "no bones" day, setting the tone for everyone watching to take it easy and get cozy—just like Noodle!

SALAD SURPRISE
TREE FROG TRAVELS BY SALAD BOX

Simon Curtis of Tulsa, Oklahoma, found a tree frog lurking in his lettuce in December 2021 and immediately fell in love with the little guy. He named the frog Tony and, after seeking advice from the Oklahoma Department of Wildlife Conservation, decided to keep him. Tony's first photo on Twitter got more than 71,000 likes, and he now lives in a big, temperature-controlled terrarium donated by a pet store.

DANCING KING
MOPSIE THE DRESSAGE HORSE

"Rave horse" Suppenkasper—also known as "Mopsie"—took the world by storm at the Tokyo Olympics after a video of his Dressage Freestyle went viral on TikTok in 2021. Ridden by US Olympian Steffen Peters, Mopsie "danced" to electronic music created especially for him by Taylor Kade, who made it to match Mopsie's moves. The music sampled the iconic "Safety Dance," among other tracks.

WORLD'S FLUFFIEST RABBIT
ANGORA RABBIT

In most people's opinion, the Angora rabbit is the world's fluffiest bunny. The breed originated in Turkey and is thought to be one of the world's oldest rabbit breeds as well. It became popular with the French court in the mid-eighteenth century. Today, it is bred for its long, soft wool, which is shorn every three to four months. One of the fluffiest bunnies ever was buff-colored Franchesca, owned by English Angora rabbit expert Dr. Betty Chu. In 2014, Franchesca's fur was measured at 14.37 inches, a world record that has yet to be beaten.

LITTLEST HORSE BREED
FALABELLA

Originally bred in Argentina, the Falabella miniature horse is the world's smallest recognized breed of horse. While newborn foals can be 12–22 inches tall at the withers (the ridge between the shoulder blades), adults mature at 25–34 inches. They are proportionally similar to other horses, and not ponies, except they are tiny; and they have seventeen vertebrae in their backbone rather than the usual eighteen. Bay (brown body with a black mane and tail) and black are the most common colors, but there are pintos, palominos, and spotted individuals resembling Appaloosas.

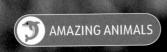

WORLD'S HAIRIEST DOG KOMONDOR

The world's hairiest dog breed is the Komondor, or Hungarian sheepdog. It is a powerful dog that was bred originally to guard sheep. Its long, white, dreadlock-like "cords" enable it not only to blend in with the flock but also to protect itself from bad weather and bites from wolves. This is a large dog, standing over 27.5 inches at the shoulders. Its hairs are up to 10.6 inches long, giving it the heaviest coat of any dog.

AMERICA'S MOST POPULAR DOG BREED
LABRADOR RETRIEVER

The Labrador Retriever holds the top spot as America's most popular dog breed for a thirty-first consecutive year. Its eager-to-please temperament makes it an ideal companion. The Labrador was originally bred as a gun dog that fetched game birds shot by hunters. Now, aside from being a family pet, it is both a favored assistance dog that helps blind people and a good detection dog used by law-enforcement agencies.

AMERICA'S MOST POPULAR DOGS

1. Labrador Retriever
2. French Bulldog
3. Golden Retriever
4. German Shepherd
5. Poodle
6. Bulldog
7. Beagle
8. Rottweiler
9. German Short-Haired Pointer
10. Dachshund

WORLD'S LONGEST-LIVED LAND ANIMAL

JONATHAN

Having celebrated his 189th birthday in 2021, Jonathan the tortoise is the world's longest-lived known land animal. He hatched in 1832 or thereabouts on the Aldabra Atoll, part of the Seychelles archipelago in the Indian Ocean. Since 1882, he's been living on a distant island in another ocean—St. Helena, part of a British overseas territory in the South Atlantic—where he was presented to the governor at the time as a gift. Today, he still lives on the lawn in front of Plantation House, the official residence of the governor of St. Helena, with three other giant tortoises. Jonathan puts his longevity down to a healthy diet of fresh grass and fruit.

WORLD'S SMALLEST DOG BREED

CHIHUAHUA

The Chihuahua is the world's smallest dog breed. It originated in the northern Mexican state of Chihuahua, and is probably a descendant of the Techichi, a mute companion dog of the Toltec civilization dating back to the ninth century CE. The breed today averages 5–8 inches tall and weighs 3–6 pounds, although the world's smallest dog ever, a Chihuahua by the name of Miracle Milly, was just 3.8 inches tall and weighed no more than a pound, not much bigger than a sneaker.

WORLD'S MOST POPULAR CAT BREED

RAGDOLL

According to the Cat Fanciers' Association, the Ragdoll melted the hearts of cat lovers in 2021. This is the third year running that the "Raggie" has taken the top spot as the most registered cat breed of the year. With its lush, silky fur and big blue eyes, this is a cat that loves to be around human beings, relaxing like a "rag doll" when curled up on your lap. The Exotic Shorthair, with its teddy-bear looks, was toppled from its second-place ranking in the listings by the Maine Coon Cat.

WORLD'S MOST POPULAR CATS

1. Ragdoll
2. Maine Coon Cat
3. Exotic Shorthair
4. Persian
5. Devon Rex
6. British Shorthair
7. Abyssinian
8. American Shorthair
9. Scottish Fold
10. Sphynx

WORLD'S BALDEST CAT
SPHYNX

The sphynx breed of cats is famous for its wrinkles and the lack of a normal coat, but it is not entirely hairless. Its skin is like the softest chamois leather, but it has a thin layer of down. It behaves more like a dog than a cat, greeting owners when they come home, and is friendly to strangers. The breed originated in Canada, where a black-and-white cat gave birth to a hairless kitten called Prune in 1966. Subsequent breeding gave rise to the sphynx.

7

INCREDIBLE EARTH

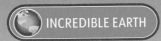
TRENDING

DEADLY WEATHER
DECEMBER TORNADOES RAVAGE KENTUCKY

Residents of eight states had a scary run-up to the holiday season as sixty-one tornadoes hit the central and southern United States on December 10–11, 2021. Eighty people died in Kentucky alone, many of them from the town of Mayfield, where a homeless man made the news for his efforts to rescue 100 candle-factory workers trapped under the rubble. December is an unusual time for tornadoes this strong, but warmer winter temperatures seem to have played a role.

DOUBLE DISASTER
AID GOES CONTACTLESS FOR TONGA

The year 2021 ended in disaster in Tonga, where a volcanic eruption triggered a massive tsunami that caused around $43.7 million worth of damage. Because of the COVID-19 pandemic, and with cases rising, Tonga was forced to ask other nations to deliver contactless aid only—meaning without human-to-human interaction or people helping on the ground.

HEAT TRAP
EXTREME WEATHER IN THE PACIFIC NORTHWEST

In June 2021, residents of the Pacific Northwest found themselves in what experts called a "heat dome"—a once-in-a-millennium heat wave trapped by high pressure. Many turned to beaches, cooling centers, or even air-conditioned hotels to cope with the conditions as temperatures soared, reaching a regional high of 121°F in Lytton, British Columbia, in Canada. As well as being an unbearable temperature for humans, the heat also had a bad economic effect, ruining wheat and berry crops.

RING OF FIRE
OCEAN INFERNO GOES VIRAL

A gas leak in the Gulf of Mexico caused an inferno dubbed the "Eye of Fire" in July 2021. Apparently, it was caused by a lightning strike hitting the gas, which had reached the surface from an underwater pipe leak. It took five hours to extinguish the blaze, in which time the internet had created memes of Godzilla rising from the ocean using stills from the viral video.

UGLY BUT AWESOME
WORLD'S LARGEST POTATO ... OR IS IT?

A tuber named "Doug" was thought to be the world's biggest potato ... until it turned out not to be a potato at all! Unearthed in New Zealand in 2021, Doug weighed an amazing 17 pounds—double the weight of a heavy human baby. Colin and Donna Craig-Brown found the giant tuber in their garden, and despite its "mutant" appearance, it tasted just like a potato. For a while they thought they had a record breaker, but DNA testing revealed that it was in fact a type of gourd. Still, Doug became a local celebrity and was even taken on walks in a little cart built by Colin.

OLDEST TREE ON EARTH
BRISTLECONE PINE

An unnamed bristlecone pine in the White Mountains of California is the world's oldest continuously standing tree. It is 5,069 years old, beating its bristlecone rivals the Methuselah (4,863 years old) and Prometheus (4,851 years old). Sweden is home to an even older tree, a Norway spruce (which are often used as Christmas trees) that took root about 9,553 years ago. However, this tree has not been standing continuous. It is long-lived because it can clone itself. When the trunk dies, a new one grows up from the same rootstock, so in theory it could live forever.

WORLD'S TALLEST TREE

CALIFORNIA REDWOOD

A coast redwood named Hyperion is the world's tallest known living tree. It is 379.1 feet tall, and could have grown taller if a woodpecker had not hammered its top. It's growing in a remote part of the Redwood National and State Parks in Northern California, but its exact location is kept a secret for fear that too many visitors would upset its ecosystem. It is thought to be 700 to 800 years old.

WORLD'S TALLEST TREES
Height in feet

- California redwood, California, US
- Mountain ash, Styx Valley, Tasmania
- Coast Douglas-fir, Oregon, US
- Sitka spruce, California, US
- Giant sequoia, California, US

379.1

327.4   327.3

317

314

LARGEST AND HEAVIEST FRUIT

PUMPKIN

The world's largest and heaviest fruit was a cultivated pumpkin weighing 2,625 pounds. It was grown by Belgian gardener Mathias Willemijns and certified in 2016 at the Giant Pumpkin European Championship in Germany. It's only the second time since 1900 that the title holder was not from North America. The seeds of most giant pumpkins trace their ancestry back to the Mammoth varieties of squash cultivated by Canadian pumpkin breeder Howard Dill in the 1980s.

AMAZON WATER LILY

The leaf of the giant Amazon water lily can grow as wide as 8.6 feet across. It has an upturned rim and a waxy, water-repellent upper surface. On the underside of the leaf is a riblike structure that traps air, enabling the leaf to float easily. The ribs are also lined with sharp spines that protect them from aquatic plant eaters. A full-grown leaf is so large and so strong that it can support up to 99 pounds in weight.

WORLD'S DEEPEST CAVE
VERYOVKINA

The limestone-rich Western Caucasus region in the Eurasian country of Georgia has some extraordinary cave systems. Among the caverns there is Veryovkina, the deepest cave in the world. It's over 7,257 feet deep! (That's more than sixteen times taller than the Great Pyramid of Giza.) It took as many as thirty expeditions over more than fifty years before Russian cavers reached the record depth, and they suspect there is even more to explore.

VERYOVKINA CAVE STATS

1968 YEAR OF DISCOVERY

7,257 DEPTH DISCOVERED TO DATE (IN FEET)

2018 YEAR CURRENT DEPTH ESTABLISHED

EXTRAORDINARY LENGTHS

In order to establish the record-breaking depths of Veryovkina Cave, cavers took three days to get down and three days to return to the surface. On both journeys, the cavers rested in subterranean camps along the way.

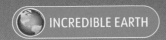
THE DEEPEST POINT ON LAND
DENMAN GLACIER

The deepest point on land has been discovered under the Denman Glacier in East Antarctica. Deep below the Antarctic ice sheet, which is 1.3 miles thick on average, there is an ice-filled canyon whose floor is 11,500 feet below sea level. By comparison, the lowest clearly visible point on land is in the Jordan Rift Valley, on the shore of the Dead Sea, just 1,412 feet below sea level. It makes the Denman canyon the deepest canyon on land. Only trenches at the bottom of the ocean are deeper. The floor of the deepest trench—the Mariana Trench—is close to 7 miles below the sea's surface.

YELLOWSTONE NATIONAL PARK

There are about 1,000 geysers that erupt worldwide, and 540 of them are in Yellowstone National Park, US. That's the greatest concentration of geysers on Earth. The most famous is Old Faithful, which spews out a cloud of steam and hot water to a maximum height of 185 feet every 44 to 125 minutes. Yellowstone's spectacular water display is due to its closeness to molten rock from Earth's mantle that rises up to the surface. One day the park could face an eruption 1,000 times as powerful as that of Mount St. Helens in 1980.

GEYSER FIELDS
Number of geysers

- Yellowstone, Idaho/Montana/Wyoming, US
- Valley of Geysers, Kamchatka, Russia
- El Tatio, Andes, Chile
- Orakei Korako, New Zealand
- Hveravellir, Iceland

540

139

33

84

16

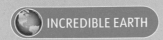
EARTH'S TALLEST MOUNTAIN ABOVE SEA LEVEL
MOUNT EVEREST

Mount Everest has grown. In December 2020, Nepal and China agreed an official height that is 2.8 feet higher than the previous calculation. The mega mountain is located in the Himalayas, on the border between Tibet and Nepal. The mountain acquired its official name from surveyor Sir George Everest, but local people know it as Chomolungma (Tibet) or Sagarmatha (Nepal). In 1953, Sir Edmund Hillary and Tenzing Norgay were the first people to reach its summit. Now more than 650 people per year manage to make the spectacular climb.

WORLD'S TALLEST MOUNTAINS
Height above sea level in feet

- Everest, Tibet
- K2 (Qogir), Pakistan/China
- Kanchenjunga, India/Nepal
- Lhotse, Tibet/Nepal
- Makalu, Tibet/Nepal

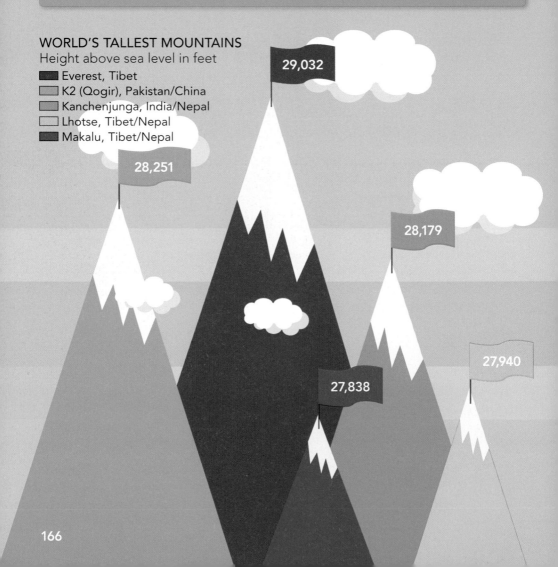

29,032

28,251

28,179

27,940

27,838

GREAT BARRIER REEF

Australia's Great Barrier Reef is the only living thing that's clearly visible from space. It stretches along the Queensland coast for 1,400 miles, making it the largest coral reef system in the world. At its northern tip, scientists have discovered a towering, blade-shaped reef, taller than the Empire State Building, that is a mile wide at its base and tapers to a knife edge about 130 feet below the surface. In recent years, climate change has posed a huge threat to the world's coral reefs, with rising sea temperatures causing areas to die off. The northern half of the Great Barrier Reef suffered particularly in 2016, and scientists fear that more damage is yet to come.

WORLD'S LONGEST CORAL REEFS
Length in miles

- ▇ Great Barrier Reef, Australia
- ▢ New Caledonia Barrier Reef, South Pacific
- ▇ Mesoamerican Barrier Reef, Caribbean
- ▢ Ningaloo Reef, Western Australia

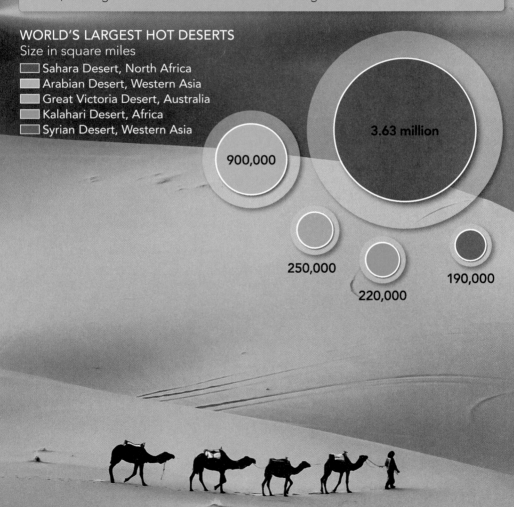

WORLD'S LARGEST HOT DESERT
SAHARA DESERT

Sahara means simply "great desert," and great it is. It is the largest hot desert on the planet. It's almost the same size as the United States or China and dominates North Africa from the Atlantic Ocean in the west to the Red Sea in the east. This desert is extremely dry, with most of the Sahara receiving less than 0.1 inches of rain a year, and some places none at all for several years. It is stiflingly hot, up to 122°F, making this one of the hottest and driest regions in the world.

WORLD'S LARGEST HOT DESERTS
Size in square miles

- Sahara Desert, North Africa
- Arabian Desert, Western Asia
- Great Victoria Desert, Australia
- Kalahari Desert, Africa
- Syrian Desert, Western Asia

3.63 million

900,000

250,000

220,000

190,000

CASPIAN SEA

Russia, Kazakhstan, Turkmenistan, Iran, and Azerbaijan border the vast Caspian Sea, the largest inland body of water on Earth. Once part of an ancient sea, the lake became landlocked between five and ten million years ago, with occasional fills of salt water as sea levels fluctuated over time. Now it has a surface area of about 149,200 square miles and is home to one of the world's most valuable fish: the beluga sturgeon, the source of beluga caviar, which costs up to $2,250 per pound.

149,200

31,700

26,600

23,000

22,300

WORLD'S LARGEST LAKES
Area in square miles

- Caspian Sea, Europe/Asia
- Lake Superior, North America
- Lake Victoria, Africa
- Lake Huron, North America
- Lake Michigan, North America

WORLD'S LONGEST RIVER

NILE RIVER

People who study rivers cannot agree on the Nile's source—nobody knows where it actually starts. Some say the most likely source is the Kagera River in Burundi, which is the farthest headstream (a stream that is the source of a river) to flow into Lake Victoria. From the lake, the Nile proper heads north across eastern Africa for 4,132 miles to the Mediterranean. Its water is crucial to people living along its banks. They use it to irrigate precious crops, generate electricity, and, in the lower reaches, as a river highway.

4,132

4,000

3,915

3,710

3,395

WORLD'S LONGEST RIVERS
Length in miles
- Nile River, Africa
- Amazon River, South America
- Yangtze River, China
- Mississippi–Missouri river system, US
- Yellow River, China

TALLEST WAVE EVER SURFED BY A WOMAN

NAZARÉ

The world's tallest surfable waves break on the Portuguese coast at Nazaré, some up to 80 feet tall. It's the place where serious surfers hang out, and in February 2020, Brazilian surfer Maya Gabeira rode a wave 73.5 feet tall. It was the highest wave of the 2019–2020 winter surf season, although Gabeira almost didn't get the chance. In 2013, she was knocked unconscious by a wipeout at Nazaré, and was found facedown in the water with leg and back injuries. After three operations to mend her broken body, she survived and is now a champion!

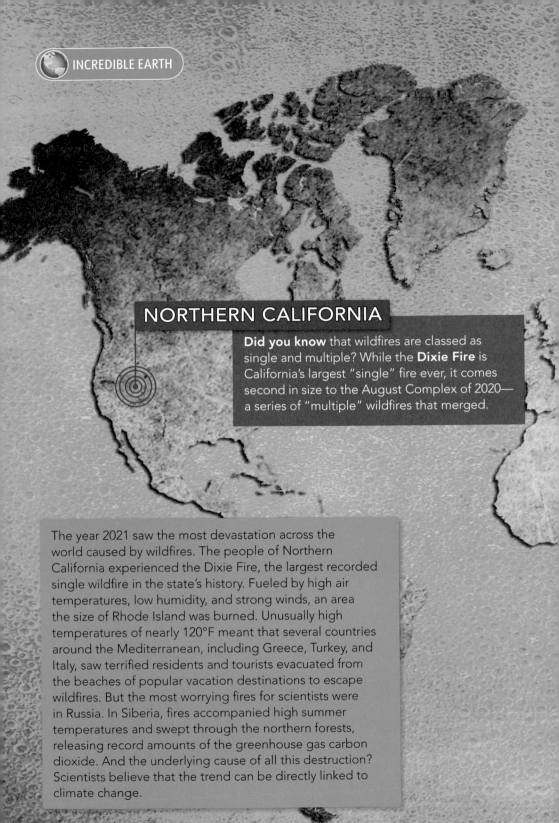

NORTHERN CALIFORNIA

Did you know that wildfires are classed as single and multiple? While the **Dixie Fire** is California's largest "single" fire ever, it comes second in size to the August Complex of 2020—a series of "multiple" wildfires that merged.

The year 2021 saw the most devastation across the world caused by wildfires. The people of Northern California experienced the Dixie Fire, the largest recorded single wildfire in the state's history. Fueled by high air temperatures, low humidity, and strong winds, an area the size of Rhode Island was burned. Unusually high temperatures of nearly 120°F meant that several countries around the Mediterranean, including Greece, Turkey, and Italy, saw terrified residents and tourists evacuated from the beaches of popular vacation destinations to escape wildfires. But the most worrying fires for scientists were in Russia. In Siberia, fires accompanied high summer temperatures and swept through the northern forests, releasing record amounts of the greenhouse gas carbon dioxide. And the underlying cause of all this destruction? Scientists believe that the trend can be directly linked to climate change.

ITALY

GREECE

SIBERIA, RUSSIA

ZOMBIE FIRES

In several locations on the Russian tundra, melting permafrost exposed peat deposits that were set alight by an increasing number of lightning strikes, releasing methane, an even more potent greenhouse gas. The peat fires, known as "zombie fires," last longer than the forest fires, and even when they appear to be extinguished, they may smolder underground through winter and flare up again the next spring.

TURKEY

MOST DEVASTATING YEAR EVER

WILDFIRES 2021

THE ARCTIC'S RECORD HIGH
VERKHOYANSK SIBERIA

On Saturday, June 20, 2020, the Arctic recorded its highest-ever summer temperature when the mercury soared to 100.4°F at Verkhoyansk, a small town in Siberia with weather records dating to 1885. This temperature was 32°F above the monthly average. It came at a time when many out-of-control wildfires coincided with a spate of unusually high temperatures in the Russian Arctic. The town has also been one of the coldest places in the Arctic, with a recorded winter temperature of –90°F, which means its inhabitants experience the greatest temperature range anywhere on Earth.

LONGEST LIGHTNING FLASH
UNITED STATES

In February 2022, the World Meteorological Organization (WMO) announced a new record for the world's longest single lightning flash, which it had discovered by scanning satellite imagery. The strike occurred two years earlier, on April 29, 2020. In the event, a 477.2-mile-long megaflash of lightning ripped through the skies above Mississippi, Louisiana, and Texas—quite a record, given that strikes rarely stretch over 10 miles. The megaflash was just 36 miles longer than the previous record holder, a 440.6-mile-long strike in Brazil on October 31, 2018.

It's official! July 2021 was the hottest month since records began in 1880. According to National Oceanic and Atmospheric Administration scientists, the global combined land and ocean surface temperature was 1.67°F above the July average of 60.4°F for the entire twentieth century, and up 0.02°F from the last record, which was first set in July 2016 and matched in both 2019 and 2020. These figures may seem small, but they are very significant and can lead to extreme weather events. The slight increase in temperature, for example, means that the warmer atmosphere carries more water vapor, which can give rise to an increasing number of powerful storms. In 2021, global tropical cyclone activity—hurricanes, typhoons, and cyclones—was down, although there was an above-normal number of named storms (tied with 1994 for tenth most since 1981).

HOTTEST MONTH EVER

JULY 2021

MOST SNOWFALL IN THE UNITED STATES
CALIFORNIA AND COLORADO

The greatest depth of snow on record in the US occurred at Tamarack, near the Bear Valley ski resort in California, on March 11, 1911. The snow reached an incredible 37.8 feet deep. Tamarack also holds the record for the most snowfall in a single month, with 32.5 feet in January 1911. Mount Shasta, California, had the most snowfall in a single storm, with 15.75 feet falling during February 13–19, 1959. The most snow in twenty-four hours was a snowfall of 6.3 feet at Silver Lake, Colorado, on April 14–15, 1921.

WORLD'S LARGEST HAILSTONE

VIVIAN
SOUTH DAKOTA

In August 2010, the town of Vivian, South Dakota, was bombarded by some of the biggest hailstones ever to have fallen out of the sky. They went straight through roofs of houses, smashed car windshields, and stripped vegetation. Among them was a world record breaker, a hailstone the size of a volleyball. It was 8 inches in diameter and weighed 2.2 pounds.

THE WORLD'S WETTEST PLACE
MAWSYNRAM

Mawsynram is a cluster of villages in the Khasi Hills of India. The plateau on which they sit overlooks the vast flatlands of Bangladesh. With 467.4 inches of rain falling each year on average, Mawsynram is considered to be the wettest place on Earth. Life here is not without its problems. Wooden bridges are washed away frequently, so locals build living bridges of knotted and interwoven roots of Indian rubber trees. Some people use a traditional "knup" umbrella in the heavy rains. Woven from reeds, this keeps the whole body dry.

STATE
STATS

TRENDING

ANIMALS CROSSING
INNOVATIVE NEW PATHS FOR WYOMING WILDLIFE

In 2021, Wyoming's Wildlife Crossing initiative enabled the state to build overpasses—bridges over busy roads—that wildlife could use to cross without danger to themselves or passing cars. Not only did animals use the bridges, but they embraced them as part of their local habitat. Officials say that collision numbers dropped by around 90 percent as a result.

FREEDOM DAY
JUNETEENTH IS OFFICIALLY RECOGNIZED

It's about time! In 2021, President Joe Biden officially signed a bill declaring Juneteenth a federal US holiday. Short for June 19th, Juneteenth commemorates the end of slavery in the United States and has been celebrated by the Black American community since 1866. On June 19, 1865, Major General Gordon Granger brought the news of the abolition of slavery to Galveston, Texas, and the first Juneteenth took place there a year later.

A GREEN OASIS
NEW YORK'S NEW ISLAND PARK

New Yorkers celebrated the end of stay-at-home pandemic rules by visiting a new city park. Little Island, designed by Heatherwick Studio and landscape architects MNLA, is built on the Hudson River at Pier 55 and opened in May 2021. Wood from the old Pier 54 was used to create a new structure, designed to look like a floating leaf, and the park hosts performers among nearly 400 different plant species.

VIRTUAL ADDRESS
ZELENSKY SPEAKS TO CONGRESS

On March 16, 2022, three weeks into a war against Russia, President Volodymyr Zelensky of Ukraine spoke to Congress via a video link from his capital city, Kyiv. Among other requests, he appealed to American politicians to help him by creating a no-fly zone over his country, to stop the Russians dropping bombs on its cities. Zelensky made a similar address to the UK government in the House of Commons.

GOING ONCE, GOING TWICE
REVERE FAMILY OBJECTS SOLD AT AUCTION

Renovators at a Boston home got a big surprise when they discovered historical heirlooms belonging to the family of Paul Revere behind an attic wall. In December 2021, these artifacts—including tools, letters, and a sign bearing the name of Revere's son—sold at auction for an amazing $20,000. The auction house expected the objects to sell for between $1,000 and $2,000, but their relationship to a Revolutionary War hero clearly put them in high demand.

STATE WITH THE OLDEST MARDI GRAS CELEBRATION

ALABAMA

French settlers held the first American Mardi Gras in Mobile, Alabama, in 1703. Yearly celebrations continued until the Civil War and began again in 1866. Today, 800,000 people gather in the city during the vibrant two-week festival. Dozens of parades with colorful floats and marching bands wind through the streets each day. Partygoers attend masked balls and other lively events sponsored by the city's social societies. On Mardi Gras, which means "Fat Tuesday" in French, six parades continue the party until the stroke of midnight, which marks the end of the year's festivities and the beginning of Lent.

ALASKA

With a total population of 725,000 people and a Native American population exceeding 145,000, Alaska is the state with the highest number of Native Americans per capita—approximately one in five. Alaska is also the state with the highest number of tribal areas, having more than 200 Native villages in total. Among the great indigenous tribes of Alaska are the Aleut, the Yup'ik, the Eyak, and the Inuit. While most live in modern communities, each tribe continues to uphold the traditions of their elders.

STATE WITH THE BEST-PRESERVED METEOR CRATER

ARIZONA

Fifty thousand years ago, a meteor traveling at 26,000 miles per hour struck Earth near present-day Winslow, Arizona, to create a mile-wide, 550-foot-deep crater. Today, Meteor Crater is a popular tourist destination and is overseen by stewards who work to educate visitors about its formation. The crater is sometimes known as the Barringer Crater, in recognition of mining engineer Daniel Moreau Barringer, who was the one to propose that it had been made by a meteorite. Previously, geologists had believed that the crater was a natural landform created over time.

ONLY STATE WHERE DIAMONDS ARE MINED

ARKANSAS

Crater of Diamonds, near Murfreesboro, Arkansas, is the only active public diamond mine in the United States. Farmer and former owner John Wesley Huddleston first discovered diamonds there in August 1906, and a diamond rush overwhelmed the area after he sold the property to a mining company. For a time, there were two competing mines in this area, but in 1969, General Earth Minerals bought both mines to run them as private tourist attractions. Since 1972, the land has been owned by the state of Arkansas, which designated the area as Crater of Diamonds State Park. Visitors can pay a fee to search through plowed fields in the hope of discovering a gem for themselves.

STATE WITH THE LARGEST NATURAL AMPHITHEATER
CALIFORNIA

Almost one hundred years since it first opened its doors to the public, the Los Angeles Hollywood Bowl remains the largest natural outdoor amphitheater in the country. The summer home of both the Los Angeles Philharmonic and the Hollywood Bowl Orchestra has a capacity for approximately 17,000 people. Many bring picnics and blankets to make the most of their music-filled summer evenings under the stars. Several events have drawn record crowds, including The Beatles, who attracted 18,700 fans in 1964, and Chris Tomlin, whose 2019 performance was a sellout. The highest attendance record of all time goes to the French singer Lily Pons, whose 1936 performance drew an incredible 26,410 people.

COLORADO

STATE WITH THE LARGEST ELK POPULATION

Colorado is currently home to around 280,000 elk, making it the state with the largest elk population. Elk live on both public and private land across the state, from the mountainous regions to lower terrain. Popular targets for hunting, these creatures are regulated by both the Colorado Parks and Wildlife department and the National Park Service. Many elk live within the boundaries of Colorado's Rocky Mountain National Park. Elk are among the largest members of the deer family, and the males—called bulls—are distinguishable by their majestic antlers.

ONLY STATE TO MANUFACTURE PEZ CANDY

CONNECTICUT

The PEZ factory in Orange, Connecticut, is the only place in the United States to make the world-famous candy. In 1927, an Austrian named Eduard Haas III invented PEZ as a breath mint. The letters come from the German word for peppermint, *pfefferminz* (PfeffErminZ). The candy came to the United States in 1952, and the company opened its US factory in 1975. Today, Americans consume an incredible three billion PEZ candies per year. The visitor center in Orange displays the largest collection of PEZ memorabilia on public display in the world, including the world's largest dispenser and a PEZ motorcycle.

STATE WITH THE MOST HORSESHOE CRABS

DELAWARE

Delaware Bay has the largest American horseshoe crab (*Limulus polyphemus*) population in the world. These creatures can be seen in large numbers on the bay's beaches in the spring. They appear during high tides on new and full moons, when they come onto land to spawn (deposit eggs). Horseshoe crabs have changed very little in the past 250 million years and have therefore been called "living fossils." It is impossible to know the exact number of horseshoe crabs in the region, so every spring, volunteers at some of the state's beaches conduct counts to track spawning activity. A full survey has not been possible in recent years, owing to COVID-19, but in 2019, the Delaware Center for the Inland Bays estimated a record seasonal count of 2,105,447 horseshoe crabs on its beaches.

ONLY STATE IN WHICH ALLIGATORS AND CROCODILES LIVE SIDE BY SIDE

FLORIDA

Where else but Everglades National Park might you expect to see both alligators and crocodiles living in the wild? The alligator is the more common of the two in America. According to the Florida tourist office, "If you don't see one during an Everglades visit, you're doing something wrong." The American crocodile is endangered, and so a rarer find. Both species like to bask in the sun on the banks of mangrove swamps and other bodies of water. The best way to tell the difference between the two is to check the shape of the snout. An alligator has a more U-shaped snout; a crocodile's is shaped more like a V. And did you know? Not only is Florida the only **state** where you can see alligators and crocodiles, it's also the only place in the **world!**

STATE WITH THE LARGEST SPORTS HALL OF FAME

GEORGIA

At 43,000 square feet, Georgia's Sports Hall of Fame honors the state's greatest sports stars and coaches. The museum includes 14,000 square feet of exhibition space and a 205-seat theater. It owns more than 3,000 artifacts and memorabilia from Georgia's professional, college, and amateur athletes. At least 1,000 of these artifacts are on display at any time. The Hall of Fame corridor features over 400 inductees, such as golf legend Bobby Jones, baseball hero Jackie Robinson, and Olympic track medalist Wyomia Tyus.

ONLY STATE WITH A ROYAL PALACE

HAWAII

Iolani Palace, in downtown Honolulu, is the only official royal residence in the United States. The palace was built during 1879–1882 by King Kalakaua, inspired by the styles of the grand castles of Europe. The monarchs did not live there for long, however. In 1893, the Kingdom of Hawaii was overthrown by US forces. Kalakaua's sister, Queen Liliuokalani, was even held prisoner in the palace in 1895 following a plot to put her back on the throne. Iolani Palace was used as a government building until it became a National Historic Landmark in 1962. Restored to its nineteenth-century condition, it is now open to the public as a museum.

Boise State
Albertsons
originally du
the "Smurf Tu
now nicknamed
Blue," was the first blue foot
field in the United States. In 19
when the time came to upgrad
the old turf, athletics director Ge
Bleymaier realized that they would
be spending a lot of money on
the new field, yet most spectators
wouldn't notice the difference. So
he asked AstroTurf to create the new
field in the school's colors. Since
the field's creation, students at the
school have consistently voted for
blue turf each time the field has
been upgraded. Today, nine
teams play on a colored
playing field, including
the Coastal Carolina
Chanticleers, whose
teal field is dubbed
"The Surf Turf."

STATE WITH THE OLDEST FREE PUBLIC ZOO

ILLINOIS

incoln Park Zoo, in Chicago, Illinois, remains the oldest free public zoo in the United States. Founded in 1868—just nine years after the Philadelphia Zoo, the country's oldest zoo overall—Lincoln Park Zoo does not charge admission fees. More than two-thirds of the money for the zoo's operating budget comes from food, retail, parking, and fundraisers. Nonetheless, the zoo continues to grow. In November 2016, it opened a new exhibit—the Walter Family Arctic Tundra—to house its newest addition: a seven-year-old male polar bear named Siku.

THE FIRST PROFESSIONAL BASEBALL GAME
INDIANA

On May 4, 1871, the first National Association professional baseball game took place on Hamilton Field in Fort Wayne, Indiana. The home team, the Kekiongas, took on the Forest Citys of Cleveland, beating them 2–0 against the odds. The Kekiongas were a little-known team at the time. In fact, the first professional game had been scheduled to take place between two better-known teams, the Washington Olympics and the Cincinnati Red Stockings in Washington, DC, on May 3. Heavy rain forced a cancellation, however, and so history was made at Fort Wayne the following day.

STATE WITH THE SHORTEST, STEEPEST RAILROAD

IOWA

At only 296 feet long, Fenelon Place Elevator in Dubuque, Iowa, is the shortest railroad in the United States, and its elevation of 189 feet also makes it the steepest. The original railway was built in 1882 by businessman and former mayor J. K. Graves, who lived at the top of the Mississippi River bluff and wanted a quicker commute down into the town below. Today's railway, modernized in 1977, is open to the public. It costs $2 for an adult one-way trip and consists of two quaint house-shaped cars traveling in opposite directions on parallel tracks.

STATE WITH THE MOST ROCK CONCRETIONS

KANSAS

Rock City, in Minneapolis, Kansas, boasts two hundred concretions of Dakota sandstone across a 5-acre park. They are the largest concretions in one place anywhere in the world. These concretions are huge spheres of rock, some of which measure up to 27 feet in diameter. They were created underground millions of years ago, when minerals deposited by water gradually formed hard, strong shells around small bits of matter in the sandstone. Over time, as the surrounding sandstone wore down, the concretions survived. Today, Rock City is a registered National Natural Landmark, and visitors can explore the park and climb the concretions for a $3 fee.

The Kentucky Derby is the longest-running sporting event in the United States. It's also accompanied by the biggest fireworks display held annually in the United States—"Thunder Over Louisville"—which kicks off the racing festivities. Zambelli Fireworks, the display's creator, says that the show requires nearly 60 tons of fireworks shells and a massive 700 miles of wire cable to sync the fireworks to music. In 2022, after having been disrupted by the COVID-19 pandemic, the live fireworks display resumed a normal program, appropriately named "The Legend Returns."

KENTUCKY
STATE WITH THE BIGGEST FIREWORKS DISPLAY

LOUISIANA

The majority of the crawfish consumed in the United States are caught in the state of Louisiana. While these critters may look like tiny lobsters, crawfish are actually freshwater shellfish and are abundant in the mud of the state's bayous—sometimes they are called "mudbugs." Before white settlers arrived in Louisiana, crawfish were a favorite food of the Native tribes, who caught them using reeds baited with venison. Today, crawfish are both commercially farmed and caught in their natural habitat. The industry currently yields more than 100 million pounds of crawfish a year, and the crustaceans are an integral part of the state's culture, with backyard crawfish boils remaining a popular local tradition.

STATE WITH THE OLDEST STATE FAIR

MAINE

In January 1819, the Somerset Central Agricultural Society sponsored the first-ever Skowhegan State Fair. In the 1800s, state fairs were important places for farmers to gather and learn about new agricultural methods and equipment. After Maine became a state in 1820, the fair continued to grow in size and popularity, gaining its official name in 1842. Today, the Skowhegan State Fair welcomes more than 7,000 exhibitors and 100,000 visitors. Enthusiasts can watch events that include livestock competitions, tractor pulling, a demolition derby, and much more during the ten-day show.

MARYLAND

The Maryland State House in Annapolis is both the oldest capitol building in continuous legislative use and the only statehouse to have once been used as the national capitol. The Continental Congress met there from 1783 to 1784, and it was where George Washington formally resigned as commander in chief of the army following the American Revolution. The current building is the third to be erected on that site and was actually incomplete when the Continental Congress met there in 1783, despite the cornerstone being laid in 1772. The interior of the building was finished in 1797, but not without tragedy—plasterer Thomas Dance fell to his death while working on the dome in 1793.

OLDEST CAPITOL BUILDINGS IN 2022
Age of building (year work was started)

1722
Maryland
250 years

1785
Virginia
237 years

1792
New Jersey
230 years

1795
Massachusetts
227 years

1816
New Hampshire
206 years

STATE WITH THE OLDEST THANKSGIVING CELEBRATION

MASSACHUSETTS

The first Thanksgiving celebration took place in 1621, in Plymouth, Massachusetts, when the Pilgrims and the Native Wampanoag people shared a feast. While the celebration became widespread in the Northeast in the late-seventeenth century, Thanksgiving was not celebrated nationally until 1863, when magazine editor Sarah Josepha Hale's writings convinced President Abraham Lincoln to make it a national holiday. Today, Plymouth, Massachusetts, holds a weekend-long celebration honoring its history: the America's Hometown Thanksgiving Celebration.

STATE WITH THE MOST LIGHTHOUSES

MICHIGAN

The state of Michigan is home to more than one hundred lighthouses—more than 120, in fact! This is hardly surprising, given that Michigan is surrounded by four of the five Great Lakes and has about 3,288 miles of coastline. As many as 1,500 lighthouses were built in the United States—most of them in the early twentieth century. Somewhat redundant today, before modern technology lighthouses were essential for guiding boats into harbors safely at night. Without them, many would have scuppered on the craggy rocks.

STATE WITH THE LARGEST MALL

MINNESOTA

The biggest shopping and entertainment center in the United States is the Mall of America® in Bloomington, Minnesota. Spread over 5.4 million square feet, with 12,000 parking spaces, it attracts 40 million people a year. As well as the 500 retail units, the mall also contains the Nickelodeon Universe indoor amusement park and an aquarium. Minnesota is also considered the birthplace of the modern shopping mall, since it is home to Southdale Center in Edina, one of the first malls, which opened in 1956.

Every four years, Jackson, Mississippi, hosts the USA International Ballet Competition, a two-week Olympic-style event that awards gold, silver, and bronze medals. The next one will be held here in 2023. The competition began in 1964 in Varna, Bulgaria, and rotated among the cities of Varna; Moscow, Russia; and Tokyo, Japan. In June 1979, the competition came to the United States for the first time, and in 1982, Congress passed a joint resolution designating Jackson as the official home of the competition. Dancers vie for prizes and a chance to join ballet companies.

It is said that America's first ice cream cone was introduced through chance inspiration at the St. Louis World's Fair in 1904. According to the most popular story, a Syrian salesman named Ernest Hamwi saw that an ice cream vendor had plenty of ice cream but not enough cups and spoons to serve it. Seeing that a neighboring vendor was selling waffle cookies, Hamwi took a cookie and rolled it into a cone for holding ice cream. An immediate success, Hamwi's invention was hailed by vendors as a "cornucopia"—an exotic word for a "cone."

MISSOURI

AMERICA'S FIRST ICE CREAM CONE

STATE WITH THE MOST *T. REX* SPECIMENS

MONTANA

The first **Tyrannosaurus rex** fossil ever found was discovered in Montana—paleontologist Barnum Brown excavated it in the Hell Creek Formation in 1902. Since then, many major **T. rex** finds have been made in Montana—from the "Wankel Rex," discovered in 1988, to "Trix," unearthed in 2013, and "Tufts-Love Rex," discovered in 2016. This last was found about 20 percent intact at the site in the Hell Creek Formation. In recent years a new exhibit named "Dinosaurs Under the Big Sky" has been installed in the Siebel Dinosaur Complex at the Museum of the Rockies in Bozeman, Montana. It is one of the largest and most up-to-date dinosaur exhibits in the world.

STATE WITH THE LARGEST INDOOR RAIN FOREST
NEBRASKA

The Lied Jungle at the Henry Doorly Zoo in Omaha, Nebraska, features three rain forest habitats: one each from South America, Africa, and Asia. At 123,000 square feet, this indoor rain forest is larger than two football fields. It measures 80 feet tall, making it as tall as an eight-story building. The Lied Jungle opened in 1992 and cost $15 million to create. Seven waterfalls rank among its spectacular features. Ninety different animal species live here, including saki monkeys, pygmy hippos, and many reptiles and birds. Exotic plant life includes the African sausage tree, the chocolate tree, and rare orchids. The zoo's other major exhibit—the Desert Dome—is the world's largest indoor desert.

NEVADA

Although it has been called the "Silver State" for its silver production, Nevada is also the state that produces the most gold. According to the Nevada Mining Association, Nevada produces more than three-quarters of America's gold and accounts for 5.4 percent of world gold production. Nevada's Carlin Trend is rich in gold deposits—and is, in fact, the world's second-largest gold resource. In 2020, two new gold deposits were found 20 miles west of Elko in the Ruby Valley. Once production starts, Nevada's gold output could rise by as much as five million ounces of gold over a decade.

STATE WITH THE OLDEST SKIING CLUB

NEW HAMPSHIRE

Nansen Ski Club, in Milan, New Hampshire, was founded by Norwegian immigrants in 1872, making it the oldest continuously operating skiing club in the United States. When it first opened, the venue only accepted other Scandinavians living in the area but was then made available to everyone as more skiing enthusiasts began to move into New Hampshire from Quebec to work in the mills there. For fifty years, the club was home to the largest ski jump east of the Mississippi, and was used for Olympic tryouts.

STATE WITH THE MOST DINERS
NEW JERSEY

The state of New Jersey has more than six hundred diners, earning it the title of "Diner Capital of the World." The state has a higher concentration of diners than anywhere else in the United States. They are such an iconic part of the state's identity that, in 2016, a New Jersey diners exhibit opened at Middlesex County Museum, showcasing the history of the diner, from early twentieth-century lunch cars to modern roadside spots. The state has many different types of diners, including famous restaurant-style eateries like Tops in East Newark, as well as retro hole-in-the-wall diners with jukeboxes and booths.

STATE THAT MADE THE WORLD'S LARGEST FLAT ENCHILADA
NEW MEXICO

New Mexico was home to the world's largest flat enchilada in October 2014, during the Whole Enchilada Fiesta in Las Cruces. The record-breaking enchilada measured 10.5 feet in diameter and required 250 pounds of masa dough, 175 pounds of cheese, 75 gallons of red chili sauce, 50 pounds of onions, and 175 gallons of oil. Led by Roberto's Mexican Restaurant, the making—and eating—of the giant enchilada was a tradition at the festival for thirty-four years before enchilada master Roberto Estrada hung up his apron in 2015.

AMERICA'S SMALLEST CHURCH
NEW YORK

The smallest church in America, Oneida's Cross Island Chapel, measures 81 by 51 inches and has just enough room for the minister and two churchgoers. Built in 1989, the church is in an odd location, in the middle of a pond. The simple, whitewashed clapboard chapel stands on a little jetty that has moorings for a boat or two. The island that the chapel is named for barely breaks the surface of the water nearby and is simply a craggy pile of rock bearing a cross.

STATE WITH THE LARGEST PRIVATE HOUSE

NORTH CAROLINA

The Biltmore Estate, in the mountains of Asheville, North Carolina, is home to Biltmore House, the largest privately owned house in the United States. George Vanderbilt commissioned the 250-room French Renaissance–style chateau in 1889, and opened it to his friends and family as a country retreat in 1895. Designed by architect Richard Morris Hunt, Biltmore House has an impressive thirty-five bedrooms and forty-three bathrooms, and boasts a floor space of over 4 acres. In 1930, the Vanderbilt family opened Biltmore House to the public.

LARGEST PRIVATE HOUSES IN THE US
Area in square feet

- ■ Biltmore House, Asheville, NC
- □ Oheka Castle, Huntington, NY
- ■ Sydell Miller Mansion, Palm Beach, FL
- ■ Pensmore, Highlandville, MO
- ■ Rennert Mansion, Sagaponack, NY

175,000   109,000   84,626   72,215   66,400

BIGGEST HONEY PRODUCER
NORTH DAKOTA

For the last fifteen years, North Dakota has outstripped all other US states in the production of honey. Currently, there are 485,000 honey-producing colonies in North Dakota, and in 2021, they produced more than 28.3 million pounds of the sweet stuff. It seems the North Dakota climate is just right for honeybees and—more important—for the flowers from which they collect their nectar. Typical summer weather features warm days but cool nights.

FIRST LAWS PROTECTING WORKING WOMEN
OHIO

NO SELF RESPECTING WOMAN
SHOULD WISH OR WORK
OR THE SUCCESS OF A PARTY
THAT IGNORES HER SEX
USA B. ANTHONY 1872 AND 1894

In the 1800s, working conditions in US factories were grueling and pay was very low. Most of the workers were women, and it was not uncommon for them to work for twelve to fourteen hours a day, six days a week. The factories were not heated or air-conditioned, and there was no compensation for being sick. By the 1850s, several organizations had formed to improve the working conditions for women and to shorten their workday. In 1852, Ohio passed a law limiting the working day to ten hours for women under the age of eighteen. It was a small step, but it was also the first act of legislation of its kind in the United States.

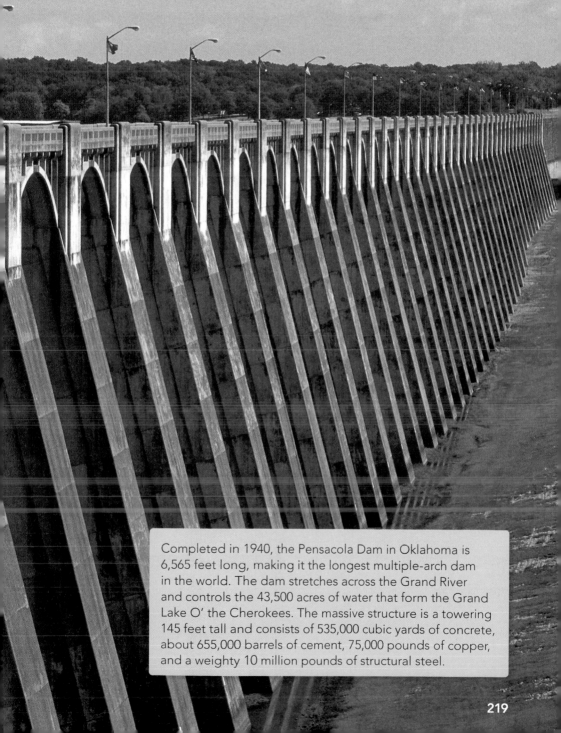

Completed in 1940, the Pensacola Dam in Oklahoma is 6,565 feet long, making it the longest multiple-arch dam in the world. The dam stretches across the Grand River and controls the 43,500 acres of water that form the Grand Lake O' the Cherokees. The massive structure is a towering 145 feet tall and consists of 535,000 cubic yards of concrete, about 655,000 barrels of cement, 75,000 pounds of copper, and a weighty 10 million pounds of structural steel.

WORLD'S LARGEST CINNAMON ROLL

OREGON

Wolferman's Bakery holds the record for the largest cinnamon roll ever made. The spiced confection measured 9 feet long and was topped with 147 pounds of cream cheese frosting. It was made to celebrate the launch of the bakery's new 5-pound cinnamon roll. Using its popular recipe, Wolferman's needed 20 pounds of eggs, 350 pounds of flour, 378 pounds of cinnamon-sugar filling, and no fewer than 220 cinnamon sticks in their scaled-up version. The 1,150-pound cinnamon roll was transported to Medford's Annual Pear Blossom Festival in south Oregon, where visitors snapped it up for $2 a slice.

STATE THAT MANUFACTURES THE MOST CRAYONS
PENNSYLVANIA

Easton, Pennsylvania, is home to the Crayola crayon factory and has been the company's headquarters since 1976. The factory produces an amazing 12 million crayons every single day, made from uncolored paraffin and pigment powder. In 1996, the company opened the Crayola Experience in downtown Easton. The Experience includes a live interactive show during which guests can watch a "crayonologist" make crayons, just as they are made at the factory nearby.

STATE WITH THE OLDEST FOURTH OF JULY CELEBRATION
RHODE ISLAND

Bristol, Rhode Island, holds America's longest continuously running Fourth of July celebration. The idea for the celebration came from Revolutionary War veteran Rev. Henry Wight, of Bristol's First Congregational Church, who organized "Patriotic Exercises" to honor the nation's founders and those who fought to establish the United States. Today, Bristol begins celebrating the holiday on June 14, and puts on an array of events leading up to the Fourth itself—including free concerts, a baseball game, a Fourth of July Ball, and a half marathon.

SOUTH CAROLINA

Pepper X, created by Smokin' Ed Currie of Rock Hill, South Carolina, is the hottest pepper in the world, measuring an average of 3.18 million Scoville heat units (SHU). To get a feel for how hot that is, just know that a regular jalapeño clocks in at 2,500–8,000 SHU. Currie also created the world's third-hottest chili, the Carolina Reaper®. The Reaper held the record from 2013 to 2017, before being beaten by the 2.4 million SHU Dragon's Breath pepper in May. Just four months after that, Currie's Pepper X took the chili pepper world by storm.

WORLD'S HOTTEST PEPPERS

By peak heat in millions of SHU

- Pepper X
- Dragon's Breath
- Carolina Reaper®
- Trinidad Moruga Scorpion

3.18   2.4   2.2   2

STATE WITH THE
LARGEST SCULPTURE

SOUTH
DAKOTA

While South Dakota is famous as the home of Mount Rushmore, it is also the location of another giant mountain carving: the Crazy Horse Memorial. The mountain carving, which is still in progress, will be the largest sculpture in the world when it is completed, at 563 feet tall and 641 feet long. Korczak Ziolkowski, who worked on Mount Rushmore, began the carving in 1948 to pay tribute to Crazy Horse—the Lakota leader who defeated General Custer at the Battle of the Little Bighorn. Nearly seventy years later, Ziolkowski's family continues his work, relying completely on funding from visitors and donors.

TENNESSEE

Tennessee is the home of the MoonPie, which was conceived there in 1917 by bakery salesman Earl Mitchell, Sr. after a group of local miners asked for a filling treat "as big as the moon." Made from marshmallow, graham crackers, and chocolate, the sandwich cookies were soon being mass-produced at Tennessee's Chattanooga Bakery, and MoonPie was registered as a trademark by the bakery in 1919. MoonPies first sold at just five cents each and quickly became popular—even being named the official snack of NASCAR in the late 1990s. Today, Chattanooga Bakery makes nearly a million MoonPies every day.

TEXAS

HYATT

If you want to see a sky filled with hundreds of thousands of bats, head to Austin, Texas, any time from mid-March to November. The city's Ann W. Richards Congress Avenue Bridge is home to the world's largest urban bat colony—roughly 1.5 million bats in all. The Mexican free-tailed bats first settled here in the 1980s, and numbers have grown steadily since. They currently produce around 750,000 pups per year. These days the bats are a tourist attraction that draws about 140,000 visitors to the city, many of them hoping to catch the moment at dusk when large numbers of bats fly out from under the bridge to look for food.

STATE WITH THE LARGEST SALTWATER LAKE
UTAH

The Great Salt Lake, which inspired the name of Utah's largest city, is the largest saltwater lake in the United States, at around 75 miles long and 35 miles wide. Sometimes called "America's Dead Sea," it is typically larger than each of the states of Delaware and Rhode Island. Its size, however, fluctuates as water levels rise and fall. Since 1849, the water level has varied by as much as 20 feet, which can shift the shoreline by up to 15 miles. Great Salt Lake is too salty to support most aquatic life but is home to several kinds of algae, as well as the brine shrimp that feed on them.

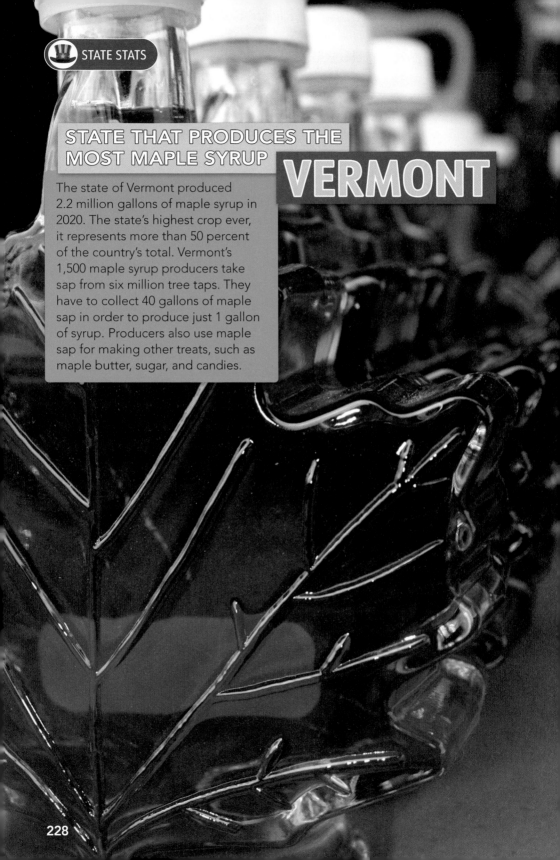

STATE THAT PRODUCES THE MOST MAPLE SYRUP

VERMONT

The state of Vermont produced 2.2 million gallons of maple syrup in 2020. The state's highest crop ever, it represents more than 50 percent of the country's total. Vermont's 1,500 maple syrup producers take sap from six million tree taps. They have to collect 40 gallons of maple sap in order to produce just 1 gallon of syrup. Producers also use maple sap for making other treats, such as maple butter, sugar, and candies.

FIRST STATE WITH WOMAN-RUN BANK
VIRGINIA

In 1903, Maggie Lena Walker opened the St. Luke Penny Savings Bank in Richmond, making Virginia the first state with a bank founded and run by a woman. A leading civil activist, Walker was also Black, making her achievement all the more remarkable in a time when the Jim Crow laws did much to restrict the advancement of Blacks in the Southern states. Through the bank and other enterprises that included a newspaper and a department store, Walker sought to provide members of the Black community with opportunities to improve their lives through employment, investment, and supporting one another's businesses.

STATE STATS

STATE WITH THE OLDEST GAS STATION

WASHINGTON

The Teapot Dome Service Station in Zillah, Washington, was once the oldest working gas station in the United States, and is still the only one built to commemorate a political scandal. Now preserved as a museum, the gas station was built in 1922 as a monument to the Teapot Dome Scandal, in which Albert Fall, President Warren G. Harding's secretary of the interior, took bribes to lease government oil reserves to private companies. The gas station, located on Washington's Old Highway 12, was moved in 1978 to make way for Interstate 82, then again in 2007 when the city of Zillah purchased it as a historic landmark.

STATE WITH THE LONGEST STEEL ARCH BRIDGE
WEST VIRGINIA

The New River Gorge Bridge in Fayetteville spans 3,030 feet and is 876 feet above the New River. It is both the longest and largest steel arch bridge in the United States. Builders used 88 million pounds of steel and concrete to construct it. The $37 million structure took three years to complete and opened on October 22, 1977. Bridge Day, held every October since 1980, is a BASE-jumping event at the New River Gorge Bridge. Hundreds of BASE jumpers and about 80,000 spectators gather for the one-day festival. Among the most popular events is the Big Way, in which large groups of people jump off the bridge together. During Bridge Day 2013, Donald Cripps became one of the world's oldest BASE jumpers, at eighty-four years old.

LARGEST CROSS-COUNTRY SKI RACE

WISCONSIN

Each year in February, Wisconsin hosts America's largest cross-country ski race. The race attracts over 10,000 skiers, all attempting to complete the 55-kilometer (34-mile) course from Cable to Hayward. Milestones along the way include Boedecker Hill, Mosquito Brook, and Hatchery Park. The event is part of the Worldloppet circuit of twenty ski marathons across the globe. The winner of the 2021 race, Ian Torchia from Rochester, Minnesota, completed the course in two hours, thirty-nine minutes, and one second to claim the $7,500 prize money.

STATE WITH THE LARGEST HOT SPRING

WYOMING

Grand Prismatic Spring, in Yellowstone National Park in Wyoming, is the largest hot spring in the United States. The spring measures 370 feet in diameter and is more than 121 feet deep; Yellowstone National Park says that the spring is bigger than a football field and deeper than a ten-story building. Grand Prismatic is not just the largest spring but also the most photographed thermal feature in Yellowstone due to its bright colors. The colors come from different kinds of bacteria, living in each part of the spring, that thrive at various temperatures. As water comes up from the middle of the spring, it is too hot to support most bacterial life, but as the water spreads out to the edges of the spring, it cools in concentric circles.

SPORTS STARS

TRENDING

RECORD BREAKER
GOLF SHOT CAUGHT
BY MOVING CAR

Talk about a difficult shot! English golfer Marcus Armitage not only won the European Tour in 2021 but also broke a Guinness world record in May for hitting a golf ball into a moving car. After several attempts (and a smashed windshield!), he drove the ball 303 yards to land in a BMW convertible, beating the previous record of 273 yards set by Jake Shepherd. No wonder Armitage's nickname is "the Bullet"!

TENNIS ACE
HIGHEST-PAID FEMALE ATHLETE

According to *Forbes*, Japanese tennis sensation Naomi Osaka was the highest-paid female athlete of 2021, with $57.3 million from both tournament prizes and endorsements. Osaka's success on the court is undeniable, but she also made headlines in 2021 for her decision to prioritize her mental health. Osaka withdrew from the French Open in May, explaining that she struggled with depression and criticizing press conferences for their effect on athletes' well-being.

GIDDY UP!
FIRST FEMALE JOCKEY WINS AT AINTREE

Rachael Blackmore, a jockey from Killenaule, Ireland, made history in 2021 when she became the first female jockey to win the Grand National at Aintree (a racetrack in Liverpool, England). She won the race on Minella Times, a horse with 11-1 odds, by six and a half lengths. Due to COVID-19 protocols, there were no spectators around to see Blackmore's record-setting win. She was later named Ireland's sportsperson of the year.

FROSTY FOOTWORK
STRANGEST SPOT FOR A KICKABOUT

In September 2021, a video of a group of Bolivian women playing soccer atop a snowy summit went viral, and the world watched in amazement as they kicked a ball around in colorful skirts despite frigid temperatures. The women were filmed playing at an altitude of 19,324 feet on Huayna Potosi mountain, in the Andes region—higher than the world record for the highest altitude for a FIFA-rules 11-a-side.

FLIGHT MODE
A DARING AND DANGEROUS STUNT

A video of motocross icon Tom Pagès went viral in 2021 after a truly amazing stunt that saw him launch himself off a cliff in Avoriaz, France. Pagès combined motocross and BASE-jumping, launching himself from the cliff edge with a 23-foot-high ramp, doing a double front flip on his motorcycle, and landing on the ground 443 feet below with a parachute. He called the gravity-defying trick "Flight Mode."

WORLD'S HIGHEST BASE JUMP FROM A BUILDING

FRED FUGEN AND VINCE REFFET

BASE jumping is just about the world's most terrifying sport to watch. BASE stands for the types of places a person may jump from: Buildings, Antennae, Spans (usually bridges), and Earth (usually cliffs). In April 2014, French daredevils Fred Fugen and Vince Reffet set a new record by jumping from a specially built platform at the top of the world's tallest building, the Burj Khalifa in Dubai. They jumped from a height of 2,716 feet, 6 inches. The highest-ever BASE jump was performed by Russian Valery Rozov on a mountain in the Himalayas called Cho Oyu. He jumped from a height of 25,250 feet and landed some 4,450 feet below three and a half minutes later.

JOCKEY WITH THE MOST TRIPLE CROWN WINS

EDDIE ARCARO

Many horse-racing experts think that Eddie Arcaro was the best-ever American jockey. Arcaro rode his first winner in 1932, and by the time of his retirement thirty years later, he had won the Triple Crown twice, in 1941 and 1948. He also won more Triple Crown races than any other jockey, although Bill Hartack has equaled Arcaro's total of five successes in the Kentucky Derby. Arcaro won 4,779 races overall in his career.

JOCKEYS WITH MULTIPLE WINS IN TRIPLE CROWN RACES
Number of wins (years active)

Eddie Arcaro	17	1932–1957
Bill Shoemaker	11	1955–1986
Earl Sande	9	1921–1930
Bill Hartack	9	1956–1969
Pat Day	9	1985–2000
Gary Stevens	9	1988–2013

WORLD'S LONGEST SKATEBOARD RAMP JUMP

DANNY WAY

Many extreme sports activities are showcased at the annual X Games and Winter X Games. At the 2004 X Games, held in Los Angeles, skateboarder Danny Way set an amazing record that remains unbeaten. On June 19, Way made a long-distance jump of 79 feet, beating his own 2003 world record (75 feet). In 2005, he jumped over the Great Wall of China. He made the jump despite having torn ligaments in his ankle during a practice jump on the previous day.

WORLD'S HIGHEST TIGHTROPE WALK
FREDDY NOCK

Tightrope walking looks hard enough a few feet above the ground, but Swiss stuntman Freddy Nock took it to the next level when he walked between two mountains in the Swiss Alps in March 2015. On a rope set 11,590 feet above sea level, Freddy took about thirty-nine minutes to walk the 1,140 feet across to the neighboring peak. The previous record had held since 1974, when Frenchman Philippe Petit walked between the Twin Towers of New York's former World Trade Center.

WORLD'S HIGHEST BASKETBALL SHOT

HOW RIDICULOUS

Australian trick-shot group How Ridiculous continues to break its own record. In 2015, one member made a basket from an amazing 415 feet, but the group has since improved that distance several times. In January 2018, How Ridiculous achieved its most astonishing feat yet: a basket from 660 feet, 10 inches. The group made the record shot at Maletsunyane Falls, Lesotho, in southern Africa, after five days of setup work and practice. How Ridiculous is a group of three friends who started trying trick shots for fun in their backyards in 2009. They now have a successful YouTube channel and business and are also involved in Christian charitable work.

NBA CHAMPIONSHIP'S GREATEST RIVALRY
BOSTON CELTICS AND LA LAKERS

NBA CHAMPIONSHIP WINS

LA Lakers	17	1949–2020
Boston Celtics	17	1957–2008
Golden State Warriors	6	1947–2018
Chicago Bulls	6	1991–1998
San Antonio Spurs	5	1999–2014

Between them, the LA Lakers and Boston Celtics have won almost half of the NBA Championship titles that have ever been played: seventeen each. The Celtics' best decade was the 1960s, when they won nine times, but the Lakers have arguably the better NBA record overall, with fifteen runner-up spots, compared to four for the Celtics. There have also been famous player rivalries, that of Larry Bird and Magic Johnson in the 1980s being perhaps the best known.

243

MOST CAREER POINTS IN THE NBA

KAREEM ABDUL-JABBAR

Many fans regard Kareem Abdul-Jabbar as the greatest-ever basketball player. He was known by his birth name, Lew Alcindor, until 1971, when he changed his name after converting to Islam. That same year he led the Milwaukee Bucks to the team's first NBA championship title. As well as being the all-time highest scorer of points during his professional career, with a regular season total of 38,387, Abdul-Jabbar also won the NBA Most Valuable Player (MVP) award a record six times.

YOUNGEST NBA PLAYER TO REACH 30,000 CAREER POINTS

LEBRON JAMES

On Tuesday, January 23, 2018, at age thirty-three years and twenty-four days, LeBron James became the youngest player in NBA history to reach 30,000 points, smashing Kobe Bryant's previous record. In 2020, James overtook Bryant in the career scoring list, just one day before Bryant tragically died in an aircraft accident. James has since passed 35,000 points, and in 2020 he collected the MVP award in the NBA Finals for the fourth time in his career.

WNBA PLAYER WITH THE MOST CAREER POINTS

DIANA TAURASI

After a standout college career and three NCAA championships with the University of Connecticut Huskies, Diana Taurasi joined the Phoenix Mercury in the WNBA in 2004. Her prolific scoring helped the Mercury to their first WNBA title in 2007 (and two more since then), and her international career includes five consecutive Team USA Olympic golds, 2004–2020. Playing mainly as guard, Taurasi became the all-time leading WNBA scorer in 2017.

MOST CAREER POINTS IN THE WNBA
Number of points

Diana Taurasi	9,174
Tina Thompson	7,488
Tamika Catchings	7,380
Candice Dupree	6,895
Cappie Pondexter	6,811
Sue Bird	6,561

NFL PLAYER WITH THE MOST CAREER TOUCHDOWNS

JERRY RICE

Jerry Rice is generally regarded as the greatest wide receiver in NFL history. He played in the NFL for twenty seasons—fifteen of them with the San Francisco 49ers—and won three Super Bowl rings. As well as leading the career touchdowns list with 208, Rice also holds the "most yards gained" mark with 23,546 yards. Most of his touchdowns were from pass receptions (197), often working with the great 49ers quarterback Joe Montana.

NFL PLAYERS WITH THE MOST CAREER TOUCHDOWNS
Number of touchdowns (career years)

Player	Touchdowns	Career years
Jerry Rice	208	1985–2004
Emmitt Smith	175	1990–2004
LaDainian Tomlinson	162	2001–2011
Terrell Owens	156	1996–2010
Randy Moss	156	1998–2012

PLAYER WITH MOST SUPER BOWL WINS
TOM BRADY

When Tom Brady joined the NFL in 2000, he was the 199th player (and the seventh quarterback) chosen in that year's college draft—hardly a potential superstar. Twenty-two seasons later, most people think of him as the greatest quarterback of all time, with seven wins and five Most Valuable Player awards heading the long list of Super Bowl records he now holds. Six of the Super Bowl wins were during his twenty-year career with the New England Patriots, but he added the seventh during his first season with Tampa Bay.

SCHOOL WITH THE MOST ROSE BOWL WINS
USC TROJANS

The Rose Bowl is college football's oldest postseason event, first played in 1902. Taking place near January 1 of each year, the game is normally played between the Pac-12 Conference champion and the Big Ten Conference champion, but one year in three it is part of college football's playoffs. The University of Southern California has easily the best record in the Rose Bowl, with twenty-five wins from thirty-four appearances, followed by the Ohio State Buckeyes (nine wins from sixteen appearances). The Buckeyes reached that second spot on the winners' list with their 48–45 victory over the Utah Utes on New Year's Day 2022.

MLB TEAM WITH THE MOST WORLD SERIES WINS

NEW YORK YANKEES

The New York Yankees are far and away the most successful team in World Series history. Since baseball's championship was first contested in 1903, the Yankees have appeared forty times and won on twenty-seven occasions. The Yankees' greatest years were from the 1930s through the 1950s, when the team was led by legends like Babe Ruth and Joe DiMaggio. Their nearest challengers are the St. Louis Cardinals from the National League, with eleven wins from nineteen appearances.

WORLD SERIES WINS
Number of wins

New York Yankees	27	1923–2009
St. Louis Cardinals	11	1926–2011
Oakland Athletics*	9	1910–1989
Boston Red Sox**	9	1903–2018
San Francisco Giants***	8	1905–2014

* Previously played in Kansas City and Philadelphia

** Originally Boston Americans

*** Previously played in New York

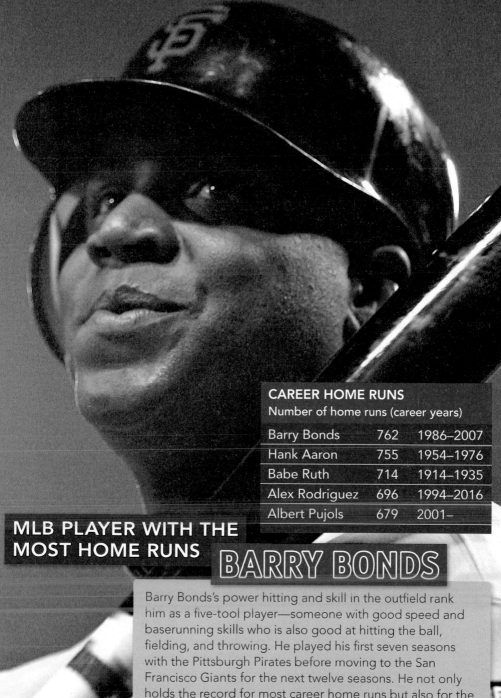

CAREER HOME RUNS
Number of home runs (career years)

Barry Bonds	762	1986–2007
Hank Aaron	755	1954–1976
Babe Ruth	714	1914–1935
Alex Rodriguez	696	1994–2016
Albert Pujols	679	2001–

MLB PLAYER WITH THE MOST HOME RUNS

BARRY BONDS

Barry Bonds's power hitting and skill in the outfield rank him as a five-tool player—someone with good speed and baserunning skills who is also good at hitting the ball, fielding, and throwing. He played his first seven seasons with the Pittsburgh Pirates before moving to the San Francisco Giants for the next twelve seasons. He not only holds the record for most career home runs but also for the single-season record of seventy-three home runs, which was set in 2001. Josh Gibson, a star of the Negro Leagues during 1930–1946, may have hit more than 800 career home runs, but the statistical records are unclear.

CHRIS WONDOLOWSKI

MLS PLAYER WITH THE MOST REGULAR-SEASON GOALS

MLS REGULAR-SEASON TOP SCORERS
Number of goals (career years)

Chris Wondolowski	171	2005–2021
Landon Donovan	145	2001–2016
Jeff Cunningham	134	1998–2011
Jaime Moreno	133	1996–2010
Kei Kamara	130	2006–2020

Californian Chris Wondolowski took a while to get his professional soccer career going. He was drafted by the San Jose Earthquakes in a late round in 2005 but didn't earn a regular starting spot with the Quakes until 2010. Since then, however, he has scored more than ten goals for San Jose every season up to 2019. He added seven more to his total in the COVID-affected 2020 season. He scored his 171st goal in November 2021 in his final professional match. He has also earned thirty-five appearances for the US Men's National Team.

WOMAN WITH THE MOST INTERNATIONAL SOCCER CAPS
KRISTINE LILLY

WOMEN WITH THE MOST INTERNATIONAL SOCCER CAPS
Number of caps (career years)

Kristine Lilly, USA	354	1987–2010
Carli Lloyd, USA	316	2005–2021
Christie Pearce, USA	311	1997–2015
Christine Sinclair, Canada	308	2000–
Mia Hamm, USA	276	1987–2004

In her long and successful career, Kristine Lilly played club soccer principally with the Boston Breakers. When she made her debut on the US national team in 1987, however, she was still in high school. Her total of 354 international caps is the world's highest for a man or woman, and her trophy haul includes two World Cup winner's medals and two Olympic golds.

COUNTRY WITH THE MOST FIFA WORLD CUP WINS

BRAZIL

Brazil, host of the 2014 FIFA World Cup, has lifted the trophy the most times in the tournament's history. Germany, second on the list, has more runner-up and semifinal appearances and hence, arguably, a stronger record overall. However, many would say that Brazil's 1970 lineup, led by the incomparable Pelé, ranks as the finest team ever. The host team has won five of the twenty tournaments that have been completed to date.

FIFA WORLD CUP WINNERS
Number of wins

Brazil	5	1958, 1962, 1970, 1994, 2002
Germany*	4	1954, 1974, 1990, 2014
Italy	4	1934, 1938, 1982, 2006
Uruguay	2	1930, 1950
Argentina	2	1978, 1986
France	2	1998, 2018
* As West Germany 1954, 1974		

COUNTRY WITH THE MOST FIFA WOMEN'S WORLD CUP WINS

UNITED STATES

FIFA WOMEN'S WORLD CUP WINNERS
Number of wins

United States	4	1991, 1999, 2015, 2019
Germany	2	2003, 2007
Norway	1	1995
Japan	1	2011

In 1991, the first Women's World Cup was held, in which the USA beat Norway 2–1 in the final. Since then, the United States has won the tournament three times more. Megan Rapinoe was named the best player of the tournament following the USA's 2019 triumph, where she scored the team's second goal in the 2–0 victory over the Netherlands in the final.

WOMAN WITH MOST GRAND SLAMS IN OPEN ERA
SERENA WILLIAMS

Serena Williams is truly one of the all-time greats in tennis, playing with a combination of power and athleticism that has made her almost unbeatable when she's been at her best. Williams first won a Grand Slam singles title at the US Open in 1999 and has since added five more, plus three in France and seven each in Australia and at Wimbledon. She's tough to beat in doubles, too. She and her sister Venus Williams have reached fourteen Grand Slam finals together—and won them all.

SERENA WILLIAMS GRAND SLAMS
Finals wins

US Open	1999, 2002, 2008, 2012, 2013, 2014
Australian Open	2003, 2005, 2007, 2009, 2010, 2015, 2017
French Open	2002, 2013, 2015
Wimbledon	2002, 2003, 2009, 2010, 2012, 2015, 2016

MAN WITH MOST GRAND SLAMS IN OPEN ERA
RAFAEL NADAL

Since Roger Federer's 2003 win at Wimbledon, three great players—Rafael Nadal, Roger Federer, and Novak Djokovic—have won sixty-one of the past seventy-six Grand Slam tennis tournaments held through early 2022. The players' domination was clearest during 2005–2009, when they won eighteen consecutive Grand Slams between them. Federer notched the trio's first success at Wimbledon and may now finally have passed his best years. Djokovic won the Australian, French, and Wimbledon titles in 2021, drawing level with his rivals for a time, but Nadal pulled in front by taking the Australian Open in 2022.

GRAND SLAM SINGLES WINS
Number of wins (years active)

Rafael Nadal, Spain	21	2001–
Novak Djokovic, Serbia	20	2003–
Roger Federer, Switzerland	20	1998–

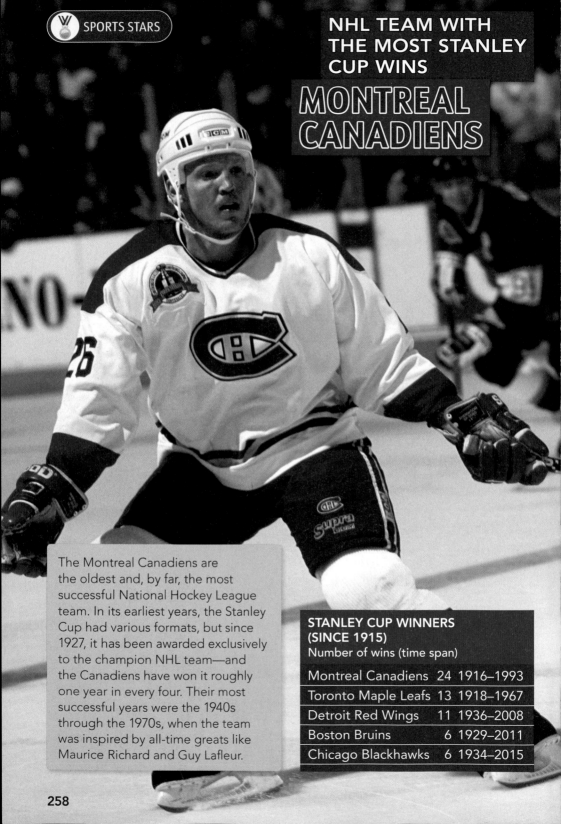

NHL TEAM WITH THE MOST STANLEY CUP WINS

MONTREAL CANADIENS

The Montreal Canadiens are the oldest and, by far, the most successful National Hockey League team. In its earliest years, the Stanley Cup had various formats, but since 1927, it has been awarded exclusively to the champion NHL team—and the Canadiens have won it roughly one year in every four. Their most successful years were the 1940s through the 1970s, when the team was inspired by all-time greats like Maurice Richard and Guy Lafleur.

STANLEY CUP WINNERS (SINCE 1915)
Number of wins (time span)

Team	Wins	Time span
Montreal Canadiens	24	1916–1993
Toronto Maple Leafs	13	1918–1967
Detroit Red Wings	11	1936–2008
Boston Bruins	6	1929–2011
Chicago Blackhawks	6	1934–2015

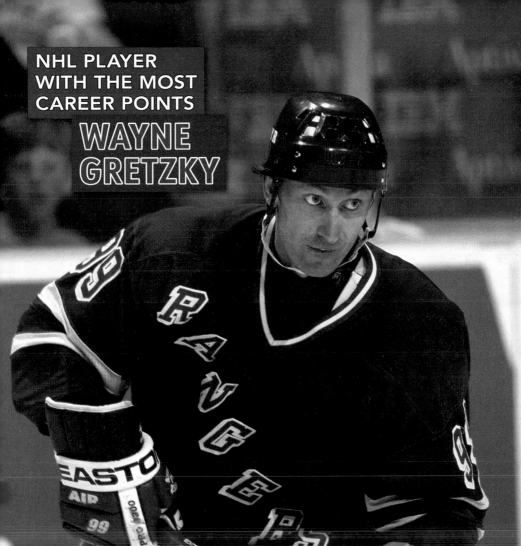

NHL PLAYER WITH THE MOST CAREER POINTS

WAYNE GRETZKY

Often called "The Great One," Wayne Gretzky is regarded as the most successful hockey player. As well as scoring more goals and assists than any other NHL player—both in regular-season and postseason games—Gretzky held over sixty NHL records in all by the time of his retirement in 1999. The majority of these records still stand. Although he was unusually small for an NHL player, Gretzky had great skills and an uncanny ability to be in the right place at the right time.

NHL ALL-TIME HIGHEST REGULAR-SEASON SCORERS	
Number of points (goals), career years	
Wayne Gretzky	2,857 (894) 1978–1999
Jaromír Jágr	1,921 (766) 1990–2018
Mark Messier	1,887 (694) 1979–2004
Gordie Howe	1,850 (801) 1946–1979
Ron Francis	1,798 (549) 1981–2004

FIRST WOMAN TO PLAY IN AN NHL GAME
MANON RHÉAUME

Manon Rhéaume had a fine career as a goaltender in women's ice hockey, earning World Championship gold medals with the Canadian National Women's Team. She is also the first—and only—woman to play for an NHL club. On September 23, 1992, she played one period for the Tampa Bay Lightning in an exhibition game against the St. Louis Blues, during which she saved seven of nine shots. She later played twenty-four games for various men's teams in the professional International Hockey League.

MOST CONSECUTIVE NASCAR CHAMPIONSHIP WINS
JIMMIE JOHNSON

The NASCAR drivers' championship has been contested since 1949. California native Jimmie Johnson is tied at the top of the all-time wins list with seven, but his five-season streak, 2006–2010, is easily the best in the sport's history. Johnson's racing career began on 50cc motorcycles when he was five years old. All of his NASCAR championship wins were achieved driving Chevrolets. He won eighty-three NASCAR races in his career, the last in 2017. He retired from NASCAR in 2020 but still competes in IndyCar events.

NASCAR CHAMPIONSHIP WINS
Number of wins (years in which the title was won)

Jimmie Johnson	7	2006, 2007, 2008, 2009, 2010, 2013, 2016
Dale Earnhardt, Sr.	7	1980, 1986, 1987, 1990, 1991, 1993, 1994
Richard Petty	7	1964, 1967, 1971, 1972, 1974, 1975, 1979
Jeff Gordon	4	1995, 1997, 1998, 2001

ALL-TIME MOST SUCCESSFUL FEMALE SNOWBOARD CROSS COMPETITOR

LINDSEY JACOBELLIS

Snowboard cross races were only invented in the 1990s, and for much of their history since then, Lindsey Jacobellis has been the dominant female athlete in the event. Coming up to the 2022 Winter Olympics, Jacobellis had won six World Championships and taken gold ten times at the Winter X Games, but her best Olympic performance, in four attempts, had been a silver in 2006, when she blew a winning lead by celebrating before she crossed the finish line. She finally got it right in Beijing, though, taking two golds for Team USA, in the individual event and the mixed team.

JACOBELLIS'S MEDAL TALLY	
Olympics	2 golds, 1 silver
World Championships	6 golds, 1 bronze
Winter X Games	10 golds, 1 silver, 1 bronze

Erin Jackson gained her first big sporting successes in in-line speed skating and in roller derby. Jackson was an in-line-skating medalist in the 2015 Pan-American Games, and it was only in 2016 that she switched to speed skating on ice. She lacked experience at her first Olympics in 2018 but did everything right in Beijing in 2022. Her winning time of 37.04 seconds in the 500-meter race gave her a 0.08-second margin of victory. There are two types of indoor ice-skating races. Long-track races in international competitions take place on a 400-meter circuit, similar in size to a standard running track. Short-track races take place on a circuit created on an international-size hockey rink. The long-track races are faster, but the short-track ones can be very dramatic, with many crashes and falls.

FIRST BLACK WOMAN TO WIN AN INDIVIDUAL WINTER OLYMPIC GOLD MEDAL

ERIN JACKSON

Nathan Chen made skating history at the 2018 Winter Olympics by being the first-ever skater to attempt and land six quadruple jumps during one performance. Quad jumps—in which the skater spins around four times while in the air—are among the hardest moves in skating, and grouping several of them in one program makes them more difficult still. Chen's record-breaking moves did not win a medal, because he skated poorly in another part of the competition, but he won the 2018 World Championship after landing his six quads once again. He retained his title in 2019 and added a third world gold in 2021. Chen finally won Olympic gold at Beijing in 2022 in the men's singles competition, though this time attempting "only" five quad jumps in his free skate program.

FIRST-EVER SKATER TO LAND SIX QUADRUPLE JUMPS
NATHAN CHEN

MOST WINTER OLYMPICS
SNOWBOARDING GOLD MEDALS
SHAUN WHITE

A professional skateboarder, successful musician, and Olympic and X Games star, Shaun White has an astonishing range of talents. He has won more X Games gold medals than anyone else, but his three Olympic golds, in the halfpipe competitions in 2006, 2010, and 2018, the most ever by a snowboarder, are perhaps his biggest achievement. The best of all was in 2018, when he landed two super-difficult back-to-back tricks in the final round to jump into first place. White's medal happened to be the USA's 100th at the Winter Olympics. White again made the USA Olympic team for Beijing 2022, just missing out on another medal with fourth place in the halfpipe. He announced his retirement from competition after this event.

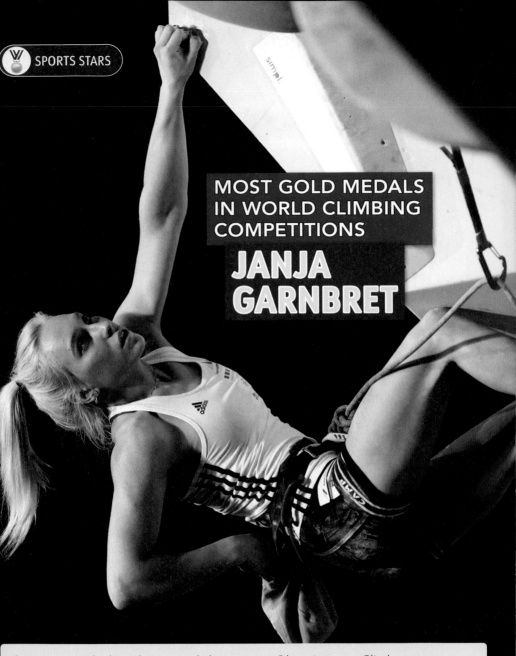

MOST GOLD MEDALS IN WORLD CLIMBING COMPETITIONS

JANJA GARNBRET

Competition climbing has recently become an Olympic sport. Climbers compete on indoor climbing walls in three disciplines—lead climbing, speed climbing, and bouldering—to arrive at a combined score for a medal. Janja Garnbret, who is from Slovenia, has won more gold medals than any other climber, male or female, in World Championships and World Cup events. She has won the combined event World Cup series every year since 2016, and over the same period won six golds at the World Championships, including all three in 2019. In 2021, Garnbret won the first-ever women's Olympic gold medal awarded in her sport; the winner of the men's competition in Tokyo was Alberto Ginés of Spain.

ARMAND DUPLANTIS

Born in 1999 and raised in Louisiana by an American father and Swedish mother, Armand "Mondo" Duplantis started setting pole-vault records when he was still in elementary school. After choosing to compete for his mother's homeland, he landed his first big win in adult competition in the 2018 European Championships. In 2019, he gained a silver medal in the World Championships, but in 2022 he moved ahead of the field in his event, setting a new world record of 6.2 meters (20 feet 4 inches). These records were in indoor competitions, but in 2020 Duplantis also achieved the best-ever outdoor jump—6.15 meters—though this is not an official world record.

MOST MEDALS WON BY AN INDIVIDUAL
MICHAEL PHELPS

Michael Phelps may be the greatest competitive swimmer ever. He did not win any medals at his first Olympics in 2000, but at each of the Summer Games from 2004 through 2016, he was the most successful individual athlete of any nation. When he announced his retirement after London 2012, he was already the most decorated Olympic athlete ever—but he didn't stay retired for long. At Rio 2016, he won five more golds and a silver, taking his medal total to twenty-eight—twenty-three of them gold.

MOST SUCCESSFUL OLYMPIANS
Number of medals won (gold)

Michael Phelps USA	Swimming	2004–2016	28 (23)
Larisa Latynina USSR	Gymnastics	1956–1964	18 (9)
Marit Bjørgen Norway	Cross-country skiing	2002–2018	15 (8)
Nikolai Andrianov USSR	Gymnastics	1972–1980	15 (7)

SIMONE BILES

Simone Biles won her first two World Championship titles in 2013 at the age of sixteen and has added to her total every season since then, apart from during a career break in 2017. Biles is only four feet, eight inches tall, but her tiny frame is full of power and grace, displayed most memorably in her favorite floor exercise discipline. She is so good that several special moves are named after her—and they are so difficult that she is the only competitor so far to perform these in championships. To date, she has won four Olympic and nineteen World Championship gold medals. Biles has also been widely praised as a champion for mental health awareness and for her bravery in speaking out as a victim in an abuse scandal in her sport.

Rio2016

SYDNEY MCLAUGHLIN

WORLD RECORD HOLDER IN WOMEN'S 400-METER HURDLES

New Jersey native Sydney McLaughlin triumphed at the 2021 Tokyo Olympics in perhaps the greatest track race of the Games. McLaughlin had set a new world record of 51.90 seconds in the US Olympic trials, edging ahead of her great rival Dalilah Muhammad. Muhammad smashed that mark with 51.58 in the Tokyo final, but McLaughlin stayed in front with an astonishing 51.46 win. No other woman has run under fifty-two seconds in this exhausting event.

FASTEST WOMEN'S 400-M HURDLES

Sydney McLaughlin (USA)	51.46	2021
Dalilah Muhammad (USA)	51.58	2021
Sydney McLaughlin (USA)	51.90	2021
Femke Bol (Netherlands)	52.03	2021
Dalilah Muhammad (USA)	52.16	2019

FASTEST MAN IN THE WORLD
USAIN BOLT

Jamaica's top athlete, Usain Bolt, is the greatest track sprinter who has ever lived. Other brilliant Olympic finalists have described how all they can do is watch as Bolt almost disappears into the distance. Usain's greatest victories have been his triple Olympic gold medals at London 2012 and Rio 2016, plus two gold medals from Beijing 2008. Usain also holds the 100-meter world record (9.58s) and the 200-meter record (19.19s), both from the 2009 World Championships.

FASTEST 100-METER SPRINTS OF ALL TIME
Time in seconds

Usain Bolt (Jamaica)	9.58	Berlin 2009
Usain Bolt (Jamaica)	9.63	London 2012
Usain Bolt (Jamaica)	9.69	Beijing 2008
Tyson Gay (USA)	9.69	Shanghai 2009
Yohan Blake (Jamaica)	9.69	Lausanne 2012

MOST DECORATED PARALYMPIAN EVER
TRISCHA ZORN

Trischa Zorn is the most successful Paralympian of all time, having won an astonishing fifty-five medals, forty-one of them gold, at the Paralympic Games from 1980 to 2004. She won every Paralympic event she entered from 1980 to 1988. Zorn is blind and helps military veterans with disabilities enter the world of parasport. Zorn was inducted into the Paralympic Hall of Fame in 2012.

LEADING PARALYMPIC MEDALISTS
Number of medals won

Trischa Zorn, USA	55
Heinz Frei, Switzerland	35
Jonas Jacobsson, Sweden	30
Zipora Rubin-Rosenbaum, Israel	30
Jessica Long, USA	29

Although China topped the Paralympic medal table at the 2022 Winter Games in Beijing (61 medals), with the United States coming in fifth (20 medals), the United States comfortably leads the all-time medal count in the Paralympic Summer Games. Norway heads the standings in the Winter Games, with the United States in third place, giving the United States an overall medal total that will be unbeatable for many years to come.

COUNTRIES WITH THE MOST PARALYMPIC MEDALS
Total number of medals won

United States	2,621
Great Britain	1,954
Germany*	1,916
France	1,276
Canada	1,247

* includes totals of former East and West Germany

TRENDING

MENTAL HEALTH MATTERS
SIMONE BILES WITHDRAWS

The United States' star gymnast drew headlines for surprising reasons at the Tokyo Olympics. Defending champion Simone Biles withdrew from both the team final and the individual competition to prioritize her mental health, after experiencing a case of the "twisties"—a mental block that could prove dangerous to a gymnast in the air. Still, Biles went home with a bronze medal for the women's balance beam and a silver for the team competition. Biles's Olympic and World Championship medal total (thirty-two in all) ties her as the most decorated gymnast of all time.

SKY'S THE LIMIT
SKATEBOARDING SENSATION WINS BRONZE

British-Japanese skateboarder Sky Brown was just thirteen years and twenty-eight days old when she won bronze at the Tokyo Olympics, making her Britain's youngest ever medalist. While she wasn't the youngest skater on the podium in August 2021, her story might be the most impressive—in June 2020, the skater and surfer suffered a 15-foot fall that ended in skull fractures and broken bones. Brown, who became the world's youngest pro skater at the age of ten, now has a huge social media following and shows off her tricks to 1.4 million followers on Instagram.

A Jamaican team has not competed in the four-man bobsled Olympic event since the famous 1988 team that inspired the movie *Cool Runnings*. But Jamaica made its return to the event at Beijing. Piloted by Shanwayne Stephens, the team unfortunately came in last out of twenty-eight teams. They were not the only surprise qualifiers from Jamaica, a nation that rarely sees snow. Benjamin Alexander, a Jamaican raised in the UK, also qualified for the alpine skiing giant slalom event—the first-ever Jamaican to compete in it.

DOUBLY A HERO
FROM COVID NURSE TO CURLING CHAMPION

Great Britain won only two medals in Beijing, both in the team sport of curling. But one of the gold medalists, Vicky Wright, made headlines for more than just her skills as the team's vice-skip—she is also a nurse at Scotland's Forth Valley Hospital. She worked in a COVID ward while training for the Olympics. The ward, where nurses and patients had cheered Wright on, welcomed her back with open arms on her first shift after winning gold—dressed in blue scrubs, with her medal around her neck.

ZAKIA'S GREAT ESCAPE
AFGHAN PARALYMPIAN REACHES TOKYO

Taekwondo Paralympian Zakia Khudadadi nearly didn't make it to Tokyo as the Taliban took over the Afghan capital and she was unable to board a plane. Trapped inside a relative's home due to the Taliban's restrictive stance on women, Khudadadi filmed a plea for help and was airlifted out of Kabul with fellow Paralympian Hossain Rasouli by the Royal Australian Air Force in time for the games. She is only the second Afghan woman to compete in any Paralympic event.

Photos ©: cover top left: Astrid Stawiarz/Getty Images; cover top right: Sarah Stier/Getty Images; cover center: Album/Alamy Stock Photo; cover center right: Collection Christophel/Alamy Stock Photo; cover bottom left: Jonathan Graziano; back cover top left: Imagespace/Alamy Stock Photo; back cover top right: Juniors Bildarchiv GmbH/Alamy Stock Photo; back cover bottom left: Joe Raedle/Getty Images; back cover bottom right: Jamie Squire/Getty Images; 4 emoji and throughout: calvindexter/DigitalVision Vectors/Getty Images; 5, 16: Photographer Group/MEGA/GC Images/Getty Images; 6 top: Kevin Dietsch/Getty Images; 6 bottom left: AFF-USA/Shutterstock; 6–7 bottom: Matt Winkelmeyer/Getty Images; 7 top: Alex Todd/Avalon/Newscom; 7 center: Jeff Kravitz/FilmMagic/Getty Images; 8: SCOTT MOORE/Shutterstock; 9: Dave J Hogan/Getty Images for BRIT Awards Limited; 10 background: Petra Urbath/EyeEm/Getty Images; 10 center: GDA via AP Images; 11: RMV/Shutterstock; 12: Jonathan Short/Invision/AP Images; 13: Chris Pizzello/AP Images; 14 background: Blue67/Dreamstime.com; 14: AP Photo/AP Images; 15: MARKA/Alamy Stock Photo; 17: John Shearer/Getty Images for The Recording Academy; 18: Rick Diamond/WireImage/Getty Images; 19: Kevin Mazur/WireImage/Getty Images; 20: Victor Chavez/Getty Images for Spotify; 21: Kevin Mazur/AMA2019/Getty Images for dcp; 22 icon and throughout: Aratehortua/iStock/Getty Images;

23, 40: Album/Alamy Stock Photo; 24 top: Lionel Hahn/Getty Images; 24 bottom: Sachyn Mital/Shutterstock; 24–25 bottom: Photo 12/Alamy Stock Photo; 25 top: REUTERS/Alamy Stock Photo; 25 center: Frazer Harrison/Getty Images; 26 background: zaricm/Getty Images; 26: PictureLux/The Hollywood Archive/Alamy Stock Photo; 27: Steve Wilkie/Cbc/ITV/Kobal/Shutterstock; 28: Casey Durkin/ABC via Getty Images; 29: TCD/Prod.DB/Alamy Stock Photo; 30: Mike Ehrmann/Getty Images; 32 background: Gaudilab/Dreamstime.com; 32: BFA/Alamy Stock Photo; 33: Chris Pizzello/Pool/Shutterstock; 34: Jim Smeal/BEI/Shutterstock; 35: AF archive/Alamy Stock Photo; 36: Courtesy of Like Nastya; 37: Panther Media GmbH/Alamy Stock Photo; 38 top: Steve Granitz/WireImage/Getty Images; 38 bottom: Taylor Hill/FilmMagic/Getty Images; 39: Joel C Ryan/Invision/AP Images; 41: Photo 12/Alamy Stock Photo; 42 background: Jimmyi23/Dreamstime.com; 42 bottom left: Simon Fergusson/Getty Images; 43: Roslan Rahman/AFP via Getty Images; 44: Bruce Glikas/FilmMagic/Getty Images; 45: Nick Harvey/WireImage/Getty Images; 46 icon and throughout: Turqay Melikli/iStock/Getty Images; 47, 51: Jeff Spicer/Getty Images for Rolls-Royce Motor Cars; 48 top: JPL-Caltech/NASA; 48 center: DigitalGlobe/ScapeWare3d/Maxar Technologies/Getty Images; 48 bottom: JPL-Caltech/NASA; 49 top: Mario Tama/Getty Images; 49 bottom: Shutterstock; 50: Jeffrey Greenberg/UIG via Getty Images; 52: Brad and Jen Campbell/

Barcroft/Barcroft Media via Getty Images; 53 bottom: Jonathan Hordle/REX/Shutterstock; 54: David Taylor/Allsport/Getty Images; 56: NASA; 57: Johns Hopkins APL/NASA; 58, 59: NASA; 60: Iain Masterton/www.agefotostock.com; 61: Hurricane Harbor Chicago; 62 icon and throughout: photosynthesis/iStock/Getty Images; 63, 76: Paisajismo Urbano; 64 top: City of Telosa; 64 bottom: Chong-Art Photography/SCA/Steven Chilton Architects 2022; 65 top: AppHarvest; 65 center: IBL/Shutterstock; 65 bottom: Lindsay Reid; 66: Yinwei Liu/Moment/Getty Images; 67: Eric Lafforgue/Art In All Of Us/Corbis via Getty Images; 68: Oliver's Travels; 69: Palacio de Sal; 70, 71: WIN-Initiative/Stockbyte Unreleased/Getty Images; 72: Beercates/Dreamstime.com; 73: Crystal Lagoons/REX/Shutterstock; 74: Su Yang/Costfoto/Future Publishing via Getty Images; 75 main: Barry Winiker/The Image Bank/Getty Images; 75 graphic: bubaone/Getty Images; 77: NASA; 78–79: Chederros/www.agefotostock.com; 80: Kajanek/Dreamstime.com; 81: Ritzau Scanpix/Sipa USA via AP Images; 82: Edward Wong/South China Morning Post via Getty Images; 83: domin_domin/E+/Getty Images; 85, 86 bottom: Justin Clemons/Guardian/eyevine/Redux; 87 top: Sanatech Seed; 87 center: Geoff Pugh/Shutterstock; 87 bottom: Dr. Rui Chen; 88: Joe Prior/Visionhaus via Getty Images; 89: Aflo/Shutterstock; 90: Seemanta Dutta/Alamy Stock Photo; 91: Stephen Chung/Alamy Stock Photo; 93: Erik McGregor/

LightRocket via Getty Images; 94: gotpap/Bauer-Griffin/GC Images/Getty Images; 95: Jay L Clendenin/Los Angeles Times/Shutterstock; 96: The Photo Access/Alamy Stock Photo; 97: Amanda Edwards/WireImage/Getty Images; 98: Normades-mond/Dreamstime.com; 100: Asiaselects/Alamy Stock Photo; 101: Stephen Lam/Getty Images; 102–103: theodore liasi/Alamy Stock Photo; 104: Kevin Mazur/Getty Images for Nickelodeon; 105: CMR Surgical; 106–107: Andreas Muehlbauer, Furth im Wald; 108 inset: Liu Jie/Xinhua via Getty Images; 108–109: GIUSEPPE CACACE/AFP via Getty Images; 109 top: PA Wire/PA Images/Doug Peters/AP Images; 109 center: Al Seib/Los Angeles Times/Shutterstock; 109 bottom: Virginia Mayo/AP Images; 110 icon and throughout: photosynthesis/iStock/Getty Images; 111, 147: Allan Hutchings/Shutterstock; 112 top: Smithsonian's National Zoo; 112 center: MasPix/Alamy Stock Photo; 112 bottom: Netflix/Moviestore/Shutterstock; 113 top: Rick Rycroft/AP Images; 113 bottom: Paul Souders/DigitalVision/Getty Images; 114: Marius Sipa/Dreamstime.com; 115: Nicholas Bergkessel, Jr./Science Source; 116: Steve Bloom Images/Superstock, Inc.; 117: Steve Downeranth/Pantheon/Superstock, Inc.; 118: NHPA/Superstock, Inc.; 120 main: Gallo Images/The Image Bank/Getty Images; 120 graphics: Krustovin/Dreamstime.com, Alenaopt2013/Dreamstime.com, filo/DigitalVision Vectors/Getty Images, Wectors/Dreamstime.com, D_A_S_H_U/

iStock/Getty Images; 121: Piotr Naskrecki/Minden Pictures; 122: Tom Brakefield/DigitalVision/Getty Images; 123: Jesse Kraft/Dreamstime.com; 124–125: WLDavies/Getty Images; 126: Bryan & Cherry Alexander/Science Source; 127: Franco Banfi/WaterFrame/www.agefotostock.com; 128: Joanne Weston/Dreamstime.com; 129: Tobias Friedrich/WaterFrame/www.agefotostock.com; 130: Ksumano/Dreamstime.com; 132: William D. Bachman/Science Source; 133: dpa picture alliance archive/Alamy Stock Photo; 134: nikpal/Getty Images; 135: Tim Laman/Minden Pictures; 136: Chris Knightstan/Pantheon/Superstock, Inc.; 137: Fabian Von Poser/imageBROKER/Shutterstock; 138–139: Bernard Breton/Dreamstime.com; 140: Piotr Naskrecki/Minden Pictures; 141: Stephen Dalton/Minden Pictures/Superstock, Inc.; 142: Roger Eritja/www.agefotostock.com; 143: Saurav Karki/iStock/Getty Images; 144 top: @mmeowmmia; 144 bottom: REUTERS/Alamy Stock Photo; 145 top: Jonathan Graziano; 145 center background: Lungchai9194/Dreamstime.com; 145 bottom: Sport In Pictures/Alamy Stock Photo; 146: Kate Kunath/Photodisc/Getty Images; 148: Mary Altaffer/AP Images; 149: Isselee/Dreamstime.com; 150: mark phillips/Alamy Stock Photo; 151 top: Hsc/Dreamstime.com; 152: Isselee/Dreamstime.com; 154 icon and throughout: Cajoer/Dreamstime.com; 155: JOSH EDELSON/AFP via Getty Images; 156–157: Tayfun Coskun/Anadolu Agency via Getty Images; 156 bottom: EyePress

News/Shutterstock; 157 top: Amanda Ray/Yakima Herald-Republic via AP Images; 157 center: EyePress/Newscom; 157 bottom: Colin Craig-Brown; 158: p-orbital/Getty Images; 159: Andrei Gabriel Stanescu/Dreamstime.com; 160: THOMAS KIENZLE/AFP via Getty Images; 161: SuperStock/www.agefotostock.com; 162–163: ROBBIE SHONE; 164: Operation IceBridge/NASA; 165: Idamini/Alamy Stock Photo; 167: Auscape/Universal Images Group via Getty Images; 168: Valentin Armianu/Dreamstime.com; 169: Jeff Schmaltz, MODIS Rapid Response Team/NASA; 170: Ahmed El Araby/iStock/Getty Images; 171: Armando Franca/AP Images; 172–173: Goldghost/Dreamstime.com; 174: Ivan Nikiforov/AP Images; 176: Edu Botella/Europa Press via Getty Images; 177: CampPhoto/Getty Images; 178: Nadine Spires/Dreamstime.com; 179: Amos Chapple/Shutterstock; 180 icon and throughout: Djahan/iStock/Getty Images; 182 top: Jackson Hole News & Guide, Bradly J. Boner/AP Images; 182 bottom: Stuart Villanueva/The Galveston County Daily News via AP Images; 183 top: Tayfun Coskun/Anadolu Agency via Getty Images; 183 center: J. Scott Applewhite/Pool via Xinhua/Getty Images; 183 bottom: Bettmann/Getty Images; 184: Dan Anderson via ZUMA Wire/Newscom; 185: Joe Raedle/Getty Images; 186: Russ Kinne/www.agefotostock.com; 188: EuroStyle Graphics/Alamy Stock Photo; 189: aznature/Getty Images; 190: Randy Duchaine/Alamy Stock Photo; 191: Newman Mark/www.

agefotostock.com; 192: Michael S. Nolan/Alamy Stock Photo; 194: Lucy Pemoni/AP Images; 195: Steve Conner/Icon SMI/Corbis via Getty Images; 197: Buyenlarge/Getty Images; 198: Don Smetzer/Alamy Stock Photo; 199: Keith Kapple/Superstock, Inc.; 200: Stephen J. Cohen/Getty Images; 201: John Cancalosi/Pantheon/Superstock, Inc.; 202: Diane Labombarbe/DigitalVision Vectors/Getty Images; 203 icons: RUSSELLTATEdotCOM/DigitalVision Vectors/Getty Images; 207: Richard Finkelstein for the USA IBC; 208: Historic Collection/Alamy Stock Photo; 209: Edgloris E. Marys/www.agefotostock.com; 210: Robert_Ford/Getty Images; 211: REUTERS/Alamy Stock Photo; 212: Nansen Ski Club; 213: Loop Images/UIG via Getty Images; 214: Visit Las Cruces; 215: Tina Pomposelli; 216: Alan Marler/AP Images; 216 graphics: siraanamwong/iStock/Getty Images; 218: Library of Congress; 219: John Elk III/Lonely Planet Images/Getty Images; 220: Courtesy of Wolferman's Bakery™; 221: Matt Rourke/AP Images; 222: Jerry Coli/Dreamstime.com; 223: Ed Currie/PuckerButt Pepper Company; 224: Sergio Pitamitz/www.agefotostock.com; 226: Fritz Poelking/www.agefotostock.com; 227: Christian Heeb/www.agefotostock.com; 228: Tara Golden/Dreamstime.com; 229: Courtesy of National Park Service, Maggie L. Walker National Historic Site; 230: Kevin Schafer/Photolibrary/Getty Images; 232: PAUL M. WALSH/AP Images; 233: Richard Maschmeyer/www.agefotostock.

com; 234 icon and throughout: Dmstudio/Dreamstime.com; 235, 263: The World of Sports SC/Shutterstock; 236 top: ALI HAIDER/EPA-EFE/Shutterstock; 236 bottom: Clive Brunskill/Getty Images; 237 top: ANL/Shutterstock; 237 center: Martin Alipaz/EPA-EFE/Shutterstock; 237 bottom: Antoine Truchet/Red Bull Content Pool; 238: ZJAN/Supplied by WENN.com/Newscom; 239: AP Photo/AP Images; 240: Streeter Lecka/Getty Images; 241: Gian Ehrenzeller/EPA/Shutterstock; 242: How Ridiculous; 243: Ronald Martinez/Getty Images; 244: Focus on Sport/Getty Images; 245: Tribune Content Agency LLC/Alamy Stock Photo; 246: Elaine Thompson/AP Images; 247: Greg Trott/AP Images; 248: ERIK S LESSER/EPA-EFE/Shutterstock; 249: Kevork Djansezian/Getty Images; 250: Jed Jacobsohn/Getty Images; 251: Denis Poroy/AP Images; 252: Scott Winters/Icon Sportswire via AP Images; 253: Guang Niu/Getty Images; 254: AP Photo/AP Images; 255: David Vincent/AP Images; 256: Adam Pretty/Getty Images; 257: Quinn Rooney/Getty Images; 258: Bruce Bennett Studios/Getty Images; 259: Rocky Widner/Getty Images; 260: Bruce Bennett Studios/Getty Images; 261: Jared C. Tilton/Getty Images; 262: Andrew Milligan/PA Images via Getty Images; 264: MARCO BERTORELLO/AFP/Getty Images; 265: The Yomiuri Shimbun via AP Images; 266: Aflo Co. Ltd./Alamy Stock Photo; 267: Oleksiewicz/PressFocus/Shutterstock; 268: Mitchell Gunn/Dreamstime.com; 269: Zhu-

kovsky/Dreamstime.com; 270: Morry Gash/AP Images; 271: Stuart Robinson/Express Newspapers via AP Images; 272: ARIS MESSINIS/AFP/Getty Images; 273: Raphael Dias/Getty Images; 274 top: Marijan Murat/picture alliance via Getty Images; 274 bottom: The Asahi Shimbun via Getty Images; 275 top: Kyodo News via Getty Images; 275 center: Lintao Zhang/Getty Images; 275 bottom: Kyodo News via Getty Images; 287: Shawn Millsaps Photography. All other photos © Shutterstock.com.

SCHOLASTIC SUMMER READING

KIDS ACROSS THE COUNTRY WORKED TOGETHER TO LOG SUMMER READING STREAKS™, UNLOCKING A DONATION OF 100,000 BOOKS!

Readers joined favorite characters and authors on Scholastic Home Base, the free, safe digital platform where they read free e-books, attended live author events, made new friends, earned digital reading milestones and rewards, and logged Reading Streaks™ all summer long!

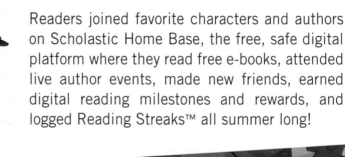

Scholastic Summer Reading 2022
Author Ambassadors

Claribel Ortega
Witchlings series, *Ghost Squad*

Justin Reynolds
It's the End of the World and I'm in My Bathing Suit,
Miles Morales: Shock Waves

Christina Soontornvat
Diary of an Ice Princess series, *The Tryout*

R.L. Stine
Goosebumps series

READING FOR A CAUSE:

By logging Reading Streaks, kids unlocked a donation of 100,000 new print books from Scholastic. Save the Children distributed the books to kids across rural America with limited or no access to reading materials.

SCHOLASTIC

HOME BASE

Join the fun year round on Scholastic Home Base!

Get ready to:

- Attend weekly live events
- Meet Scholastic authors
- Play games and discover books
- Interact with your favorite characters
- Chat with other fans
- Play on your computer, phone, or tablet
- And more!

Home Base is free and moderated 24/7 for safety!

HOME BASE
SCHOLASTIC

Download the **Home Base** app or go to
scholastic.com/homebase